KING HENRY IV, PART 2

NOTES

including
- *Introduction*
- *Scene-by-Scene Synopses*
- *Commentaries*
- *Suggested Questions*
- *Character Sketches*
- *Critical Notes*
- *Selected Bibliography*

by
James K. Lowers, Ph.D.
Department of English
University of Hawaii

INCORPORATED

LINCOLN, NEBRASKA 68501

Editor

Gary Carey, M.A.
University of Colorado

Consulting Editor

James L. Roberts, Ph.D.
Department of English
University of Nebraska

ISBN 0-8220-0026-1
© Copyright 1963
by
C. K. Hillegass
All Rights Reserved
Printed in U.S.A.

1990 Printing

The Cliffs Notes logo, the names "Cliffs" and "Cliffs Notes," and the black and yellow diagonal-stripe cover design are all registered trademarks belonging to Cliffs Notes, Inc., and may not be used in whole or in part without written permission.

Cliffs Notes, Inc.   Lincoln, Nebraska

CONTENTS

INTRODUCTION

It is apparent that Shakespeare planned both parts of *Henry IV* at the same time. In Holinshed's *Chronicles of England, Scotland, and Ireland* (1587 ed.), the chief source for his English chronicle history plays, he found the story of three rebellions against the English King. He chose to reduce these to two phases of a single rebellion. For the action relating to Prince Hal and the Lord Chief Justice, Shakespeare depended upon Sir Thomas Elyot's account in *The Book Called the Governour* (1531) and an old play entitled *The Famous Victories of Henry V. Henry IV, Part I,* was published in 1598, and that is the date accepted for the composition of the second part. An indication of its popularity is the fact that a quarto edition of the play was printed two years later after successful performances.

The first play ended with the royal victory over the rebels at Shrewsbury. "Thus ever did rebellion find rebuke" were the words of the King. But in the north parts of England civil war threatened, and King Henry ordered John of Lancaster and the Earl of Westmoreland to lead forces "against Northumberland and the prelate Scroop"—that is, against Hotspur's father and the disgruntled Archbishop of York. It is at this point that the second part of the play begins.

Shakespeare's source did not provide him with such a figure as the gallant, impetuous Hotspur, who, as adversary of Prince Hal, made possible effective dramatic contrast and an exciting climax and resolution to the action. John of Lancaster, not Prince Hal, leads the King's forces against the rebels in this play. He defeats them by means of a ruse, not through valor. Prince Hal flourishes especially in the comic subplot throughout most of the play. Yet since the young Prince is to succeed his father and to become the Hero King of England, his role in the comic scenes is diminished appreciably toward the end, for Shakespeare carefully prepared the way to the rejection of Falstaff.

If there is no great foe like Hotspur in the main plot, it nevertheless has its own facets of interest. Chief among these is the attention given to the King's relation with Prince Hal. In scenes replete with irony, the conscious-stricken father is never able to push from his mind the knowledge that he was a usurper, and he misunderstands entirely the motives and actions of his son and heir. Audiences agree that the King's suffering has been movingly realized.

Falstaff, one of the most complex characters in literature, remains a superb comic creation. If anything, he is even less repressed. Poins, Bardolph of the flaming nose, and Peto reappear— the first as Prince Hal's companion at the Boar's-Head Tavern, the other two as cronies of Falstaff. Joining them is a new comic figure, the swaggering Pistol, whose explosive discourse fails to conceal his cowardice. Not only does Mistress Quickly, hostess of the Boar's-Head, find a place in the play, but her role is wonderfully developed. Thanks especially to her genius for misusing words, she makes a notable contribution to the broad comedy of the subplot. With her is another new character, the unrestrained Doll Tearsheet, whose startling vocabulary rivals that of Pistol, if in a different way.

But this is not all. In Act III, Shakespeare introduces two other original comic characters. These are two country justices-of-the-peace, the vain Shallow and Silent, his naive kinsman and admirer. The scenes in which these two appear hold their own with any others in the *Henry IV* plays for sheer hilarity.

If some are less satisfied with *Henry IV, Part II,* it is primarily because of the fate of Falstaff. In a memorable speech in the earlier play (II.iv.521) he had addressed these words to Prince Hal:

No, my good lord. Banish Peto, banish Bardolph, banish Poins. But for sweet Jack Falstaff, kind Jack Falstaff, valiant Jack Falstaff, and therefore more valiant, being old Jack Falstaff, banish not him thy Harry's company, banish not him thy Harry's company. Banish plump Jack, and banish all the world.

Yet he is banished. "I know thee not, old man," says the newly crowned Henry V. And these words seem heartless when spoken to that very embodiment of mirth, the man who was not only witty in himself but the cause that wit is in other men. The judicious reader, however, will recall that, basically, this is a play about rebellion—about disorder—in the State. Without failing to be vastly amused by Falstaff, he nevertheless will recognize that plump Jack *is* a rebel against order. That so many should lament the fate of Falstaff is one of the finest tributes to Shakespeare's ability to create a character who seems actually to live. Legend has it that Queen Elizabeth I herself was so amused by Sir John that she urged Shakespeare to write another play in which the knight would trod the boards once more.

INDUCTION

The induction, a device rarely used by Shakespeare, is a forty-line prologue which serves to link the two parts of *Henry IV*. It is spoken by Rumour, an allegorical figure who appears before Wark-worth Castle in Northumberland "painted full of tongues," as described in part by Virgil *(Aeneid,* IV. 174). Rumour's function is to confuse all and sundry as to what actually was the outcome of the Battle of Shrewsbury. At first Rumour tells the truth: King Henry's forces had crushed the rebels. Then Rumour spread false reports: Hotspur killed Harry Monmouth (Prince Hal); the Earl of Douglas subdued King Henry; the rebels won an overwhelming victory.

ACT I – SCENE I

SYNOPSIS

This scene first reveals how well Rumour has done its work. The setting is Warkworth Castle, seat of the House of Percy, the head of which is the Earl of Northumberland, who had remained "crafty sick" at home, rather than joining his son and brother at Shrewsbury. Lord Bardolph arrives and jubilantly tells Northumberland that the rebel forces commanded by the Earl's son have triumphed. According to him King Henry was wounded and is near death; Henry Percy had slain Prince Hal and taken prisoner John of Lancaster; the Earl of Douglas had killed Sir Walter Blunt. Northumberland is assured that this information came from "a gentleman well bred and of good name," who had just come from the site of the battle. At this moment Travers arrives with a far different story which he had learned from another who claimed to have been an eye-witness. His report is that the rebels suffered a crushing defeat and that Northumberland's son had been killed. Although Lord Bardolph is willing to wager his barony on the truth of his report the Earl does not know which to believe. All doubts are settled when Morton arrives direct from Shrewsbury and gives his first-hand account. The King had indeed triumphed. Hotspur had been slain; the Earls of Worcester and Douglas are captives. Moreover, Morton states that even now John of Lancaster and the Earl of Westmoreland lead troops against Northumberland and his faction.

For a moment the Earl gives way to stormy passion. But Travers and Lord Bardolph urge caution and restraint. Morton in particular advises him to remember how many lives are at stake and how necessary it is to wait until a large force is mobilized. A telling point is his reminding Northumberland of the great risk Hotspur had taken with his father's approval. But there is no question of flight. Lord Bardolph concedes that, in the first venture, the risk was great, but points out that the possibility of gain was no less great. In ringing words he voices the sentiments of all: "Come, we will all put forth, body and goods." Morton is quick to concur, for now he has good news. The Archbishop of York has raised a force to oppose King Henry. Northumberland states that he was aware of the powerful Archbishop's activities, and he directs his followers to waste no time in seeking the best counsel in order to insure safety and revenge.

CHARACTERS IN SCENE 1

THE EARL OF NORTHUMBERLAND—Henry Percy the elder, father of Hotspur. As leader of the House of Percy, the most powerful baronial family in northern England, he had led the triumvirate which included his brother and his son in support of Henry Bolingbroke and was largely responsible for placing Henry on the throne. Later, he and his faction accused the King of failing to keep his promises to them and rose in revolt. Pleading illness, he had absented himself from the battlefield at Shrewsbury and had survived to threaten the King with rebellion once more.

LORD BARDOLPH—Thomas Bardolph, a noble mentioned by Holinshed, who is a leading member of the Percy faction.

TRAVERS AND MORTON—Two loyal retainers of the Earl of Northumberland who, like so many in the north parts of England, "knew no Prince but a Percy."

CHARACTERS NOT PRESENT BUT MENTIONED

KING HARRY—King Henry IV (also referred to as Bolingbroke, a place name), son of John of Gaunt and grandson of Edward III. In deposing and succeeding Richard II he founded the Lancastrian dynasty of English rulers.

PRINCE HARRY—Prince Hal (also referred to as Harry Monmouth), son and heir to Henry IV, who, after apparent disregard of his princely obligations, had emerged the hero of the Battle of Shrewsbury.

DOUGLAS—Archibald, fourth Earl of Douglas and first Duke of Touraine. A famous Scottish warrior, he was first an enemy and then an ally of Hotspur. Captured by the royal forces at Shrewsbury he lived to become a supporter of Henry V in the French wars.

WESTMORELAND—Ralph Neville, Earl of Westmoreland

and brother-in-law to the King. He had opposed Richard II and had assisted at the coronation of Henry IV.

SIR JOHN—None other than Falstaff, who dominates the comic scenes in both parts of *Henry IV*. Interestingly enough, he is here identified as one of the most important leaders of the royalist forces.

WORCESTER—Thomas Percy, the wily Earl of Worcester, brother of Northumberland, who fought with his nephew, Hotspur, at Shrewsbury.

ARCHBISHOP OF YORK—Richard Scroop (Richard Le Scrope), who had attained his high office at the request of Richard II. Although he supported Henry IV for a time, early in that King's reign he issued an indictment of the government and raised a body of supporters.

SIR WALTER BLUNT—A stalwart Lancastrian and friend of John of Gaunt, Henry IV's father. He was a minor but useful character in *Henry IV, Part I*, serving principally as the King's emissary.

PURPOSE OF THE SCENE

1. To establish the basic theme of the main plot.
2. To clarify the relationship between the first and second parts of *Henry IV*.
3. To introduce the leader of the rebellious Percy faction and to identify important adherents to their cause.
4. To provide the inciting incident which, in a technical sense, starts the action rising toward its climax.
5. To impress upon the audience the momentousness of the issues involved—the new dangers which now face Henry IV and all England.

SUGGESTED QUESTIONS

1. In lines 20-23, exactly what does Lord Bardolph mean by reference to "Caesar's fortunes"?
2. How may one paraphrase lines 60-61?
   Yea, this man's brow, like a title leaf,
   Foretells the nature of a tragic volume.
3. What is meant by the reference to the Archbishop of York as a man "with double surety"?

ACT I – SCENE 2

The opening dialogue between Falstaff and his newly acquired page deals successively with the latter's report on three matters and with Falstaff's reaction to each report. The first is the doctor's diagnosis of the knight's physical condition, which is hardly flattering. Falstaff, remarking that many take pride in gibing him, cites the latest prank played on him by Prince Hal—sending him the page whose dimunitiveness offers such a comic contrast to the fat knight. But Falstaff, never at loss for words, expresses his views at length, concluding that the Prince is now almost out of grace with him. Next, the page says that the tailor from whom Falstaff had ordered twenty yards of satin has refused to honor the knight's credit, particularly when Bardolph was his security. Finally, the page reports that Bardolph has gone to buy Falstaff a horse. And this bit of intelligence gives Sir John another chance to display his wit.

At this point the little page announces the arrival of the Lord Chief Justice of England, identifying him as the man who had sent the Prince to prison for attempting to circumvent justice on behalf of Bardolph after the Gadshill robbery (see *Henry IV, Part I,* Act II). Falstaff pretends that his new appointment as a commander of troops moving against the northern rebels makes it impossible for him to concern himself with other matters. But the Chief Justice will not be put off. As he reproves the knight for ignoring his summons to appear before him, Falstaff attempts to avoid the issue by expressing concern for the Justice's health and then, at greater length, for the King's—even going so far as to offer a diagnosis. In so many words, Falstaff is denounced as a wastrel, as one who has misled the young Prince, and as one who defies convention and the principle of decorum befitting an elderly man. All this serves only to inspire audacious, witty replies. Falstaff concedes that Prince Hal should not have boxed the ears of the Lord Chief Justice, adds that he had "checked him for it," and concludes that the Prince remains unconcerned, as obviously does Falstaff himself. Then he confirms the report that he has been asked to serve his King once more by joining the royal forces against the Archbishop of York and the Earl of Northumberland. And when the Chief Justice gives his blessings on the enterprise, Sir John brazenly asks him for the loan of a thousand pounds.

Alone with the page, Falstaff voices a complaint on his near-empty purse. In order to raise money, he sends the page with letters to John of Lancaster, to Prince Hal, and to "old Mistress Ursula," whom he weakly had promised to marry. As he concludes, "A good wit will make use of anything."

CHARACTERS IN SCENE 2

FALSTAFF—Sir John, the most famous comic character of Shakespearean drama who has won a place in the company of Prince Hal because of his matchless wit and incessant gaiety, his unfailing ability to incite laughter. Indeed, so gifted is he that generations of audiences have taken him to their hearts, often refusing to believe that he has any basic shortcomings and that his derelictions are all part of a game he plays for the sake of merriment. It may be argued that, in a sense, Falstaff embodies the rebel against seriousness and authority which is latent in many of the most respectable people. Grossly fat, white bearded, he appears as the very spirit of irresponsible youth. His final line in this scene very well sums up his philosophy of life.

LORD CHIEF JUSTICE OF THE KING'S BENCH— England's premier legal official, an elderly, sober, dedicated man intent on seeing to it that order and justice in civil life are maintained within the realm. In this scene he functions as a foil to Falstaff and helps to provide the link between the first and second parts of *Henry IV.*

THE PAGE—The witty little servant, a present to Falstaff from Prince Hal.

CHARACTERS NOT PRESENT BUT MENTIONED

BARDOLPH—Falstaff's serving man and one of the habitues of the Boar's-Head Tavern. Memorable for his bright red nose, he was the source of good comedy of physical appearance in the earlier play.

JOHN OF LANCASTER—Prince John, Duke of Lancaster, third son of Henry IV and general of the royal forces sent against the northern insurgents.

ARCHBISHOP OF YORK—Richard Scroop, powerful leader of the malcontents in Yorkshire.

EARL OF NORTHUMBERLAND—Henry Percy the elder, leader of the Percy faction opposed to Henry IV.

PRINCE HAL—Henry, heir apparent to the throne of England who, after the Battle of Shrewsbury, had joined his royal father in the Welsh wars.

PURPOSE OF THE SCENE

1. To start the subplot and introduce the theme of order therein.
2. To present a full-length portrait of Falstaff.
3. To make clear the fact that, despite the King's injunction, Falstaff and Prince Hal will soon appear together again.
4. To keep to the fore the major theme of rebellion and thus to link main plot and subplot, which is not to be considered as mere "comic relief."

SUGGESTED QUESTIONS

1. What facets of Falstaff's character are clearly revealed in this scene?
2. What does the servant exactly mean when he says, "I pray you, sir, then set your knighthood and your soldiership aside and give me leave to tell you you lie in your throat..." (lines 95-97)?
3. In addition to trying to evade the Chief Justice's reprimands, what is a probably explanation of Falstaff's concern for the King's health?

ACT I – SCENE 3

SYNOPSIS

Present at the Palace of Richard Scroop, Archbishop of York, are the Archbishop himself, Lord Hastings, Mowbray (Earl Marshal of the North Parts), and Lord Bardolph. This is a council of war to determine the course of events. The Archbishop has explained the reason for the move against the King and indicated what forces are at his disposal. Mowbray, at one with Scroop as regards grievances, questions that the insurgents are strong enough to oppose the King. Lord Hastings reports that already 25,000 men have been mustered and that reenforcements from Northumberland are expected. Judiciously, Lord Bardolph points out that the basic question is whether or not the rebels can survive without reenforcements. His own position is that it would be foolhardy for the rebels to commit themselves until they are sure of Northumberland's help. The Archbishop agrees: they must not make the fatal mistake which Hotspur made at Shrewsbury. It is Lord Bardolph who sums up the argument, emphasizing the fact that they seek "almost to pluck a kingdom down/ And set up another." Caution, he concludes, must be the watchword.

But Lord Hastings argues that the present force is large enough, and he has good reasons to support his case. King Henry faces danger from the French and from the Welsh led by Glendower, as well as from the northern insurgents: "So is the unfirm King/ In three divided." Moreover, Hastings reports that the Royal treasury is depleted.

This argument seems irrefutable. It is agreed that Henry IV cannot possibly commit all his forces against the Scroop-Percy faction and leave the realm defenseless against the Welsh and the French. Once more the audience learns that the Duke (John of Lancaster) and the Earl of Westmoreland lead the royalists northward, and the King and Harry of Monmouth (Prince Hal) will move against the Welsh. Who will oppose the French, if they should attack England, is not known.

The Archbishop then urges that the insurgents publish their list of grievances in which the King's government will be indicted for misrule. Both Mowbray and Hastings, fired with enthusiasm, call for prompt action: "We are time's subjects, and time bids be gone."

CHARACTERS IN SCENE 3

ARCHBISHOP OF SCROOP—Richard Scroop, to whom important reference was made in Scene 1. Here he emerges as a powerful opponent of Henry IV. He has been able to muster a force of 25,000 men. If one recalls that Henry V led a force of only 15,000 against the French, and that Henry VIII's forces opposing the rebels of 1536 numbered less than 9,000 men, he can appreciate the seriousness of the threat against the Crown. The Archbishop wisely invites and listens to contrary points of view before making up his own mind on what action should be taken.

MOWBRAY—Thomas, second Duke of Norfolk. He was the elder son of Thomas Mowbray, first Duke of Norfolk, who had been banished by Richard II because of his quarrel with Henry Bolingbroke, the man who now rules England. Perhaps because, for a time, he had been excluded from his father's honors, he joined the Archbishop and the Percies in the treasonable action of the year 1405. Anything but foolhardy, he is a determined, strong adversary.

LORD BARDOLPH—His adherence to the Percy cause having been well established in Scene 1, he now represents the

Earl of Northumberland and shares the latter's sense of caution.

LORD HASTINGS — Sir Edward, eighth Lord Hastings, scion of an important baronial family which had included Earls of Pembroke. The fifth Lord Hastings had married Philippa, daughter of Edmund Mortimer, Earl of March, to whom Richard II had willed the Crown of England.

PURPOSE OF THE SCENE

1. To advance the main plot by presenting the council of rebel leaders, who, after an estimate of all factors, voice their determination to take to the field.

2. To introduce personally the powerful Archbishop of York, co-leader of the northern insurgents.

3. To make even clearer the grave dangers confronting King Henry IV: the odds are weighted heavily against him in view of the threats from Wales and France.

SUGGESTED QUESTIONS

1. Exactly how did Hotspur "line himself with hope," in the words of Lord Bardolph (line 27)?

2. What does Lord Bardolph mean by the term *winking* in his reference to Hotspur (line 33)?

3. How may one paraphrase and explain lines 87-88?

> The commonwealth is sick of their own choice,
> Their overgreedy love hath surfeited.

A C T   I I — S C E N E   1

SYNOPSIS

On a London street Mistress Quickly, Hostess of the Boar's-Head Tavern, asks Fang, the Sheriff's sergeant, whether or not he has served notice of the legal action she has brought against Falstaff. He assures her that he has done so. Snare, the Sergeant's man, appears on call and is ordered to arrest the knight. When Snare voices concern for his life, the Hostess urges caution. In lines packed with *double-entendre* hardly complimentary to her own character and to Falstaff's, she recalls how she had been victimized. Vocally, at least, Fang is all courage and determination; he "cares not his (Falstaff's) thrust."

The Hostess fills in the details in lines marked by the repeated misuse of words. Falstaff, she insists, owes her one hundred marks (about seventy-eight pounds). He may be expected to appear in one of three public places. And at this moment Falstaff indeed appears, along with Bardolph and the page.

Falstaff demands to know what all the fuss is about: "Whose mare's dead?" Fang promptly declares him to be under arrest. Lively action ensues. Falstaff calls upon Bardolph to cut off Fang's head and to throw the Hostess in the gutter. First crying out "Murder! Murder!" Mistress Quickly then adds her voice to that of Fang in an appeal to passers-by for help—although it would seem that she is doing very well without assistance. The page adds to the din, scurrilously denouncing her, just as the Chief Justice and his men arrive on the scene.

The Chief Justice upbraids Sir John for street brawling, particularly at a time when he should be hurrying to join the royalists in Yorkshire. He is then told that Falstaff has imposed grievously upon Mistress Quickly, using worthless promises as the coin of the realm. Asked if he is not ashamed of himself for imposing upon a poor widow, Falstaff calmly asks the Hostess for a bill of particulars. A new charge against him is included in her reply: as she had dressed the head wound he had received from Prince Hal for insulting the King, he had promised to marry her, had even kissed her—and had borrowed thirty shillings.

Falstaff assures the Chief Justice that the poor woman is demented, in proof whereof he states that she had declared her oldest son to be the very image of the Chief Justice. How to account for her sad state? Once prosperous, now indigent, she had lost her wits. Magnanimously, he does not bring charges against her. But as for Fang and Snare, that is a different matter.

The Chief Justice refuses to be misled by what he calls Falstaff's "impudent sauciness," pointing out that long since he has been familiar with the knight's behavior. He orders that Falstaff make restitution and mend his ways.

Sir John, unmistakably irritated by this "sneap" (insult), as he calls it, moves to the attack. He is not impudent; he is honorably bold. Nor will he curtsey to the Chief Justice or deign to be a suitor. Instead, he claims immunity on the grounds that he is engaged in the urgent business of the King.

As the Chief Justice firmly tells Falstaff to pay his debt, Gower, a messenger, enters with news for England's leading legal official: the King and Harry, Prince of Wales, are near London.

Falstaff and the Hostess hold the center of the stage while the two converse.

Now Falstaff uses all his wit and gives the audience a demonstration of his skill in victimizing the Hostess and, incidentally, substantiates her charges against him. He succeeds in getting her to agree to sell treasured furnishings of the tavern in order to raise money for him. "Will you pay me altogether," she asks, not without pathos. "As I live," replies Falstaff, and in an aside he instructs Bardolph to go with her and see that she does not change her mind. Before she leaves, however, she agrees to have Doll Tearsheet join the knight at the Boar's-Head, where he will continue to indulge himself and stretch his credit.

Falstaff and the Chief Justice now remain alone on stage. In their final exchange, it is revealed that the King has sent 1500 foot troops and 500 horses to augment the force led by the Duke of Lancaster. Falstaff is unable to learn whether or not the King plans to return to London at once.

Patently ignoring the Chief Justice, Sir John twice asks Gower, the messenger, to dine with him. The Chief Justice reproves him for loitering in London streets at a time of national peril and for a display of bad manners. Voicing his pride in his ability at verbal dueling, Falstaff says in effect that the Chief Justice had been his teacher as far as manners were concerned. "Thou art a great fool," replies the latter as the scene ends.

CHARACTERS IN SCENE 1

THE HOSTESS—Mistress Quickly, the credulous, kindly hostess of the Boar's-Head Tavern, who has been victimized by Falstaff in more ways than that relating to pounds, shillings, and pence. A devout lover of long words, she has her difficulty in getting them right and thus provides first-rate comedy of words. She strives to hang on to some reputation for respectability, insisting that Falstaff had promised to marry her and using such phrases as "saving your manhoods" (line 29), which were usually voiced after inadvertently making an improper remark.

MASTER FANG—The Sheriff's sergeant, charged with the duty of delivering notices of action in civil cases and insuring the appearance of the accused in court. The obtuse Fang repeatedly strives to impress others with his efficiency and courage.

SNARE—The Sergeant's assistant, whose timidity provides a comic contrast to the apparent valor of his superior. Like Fang, and for that matter most of Shakespeare's characters at this social level, he is a realistic, well-delineated individual, despite his minor role.

FALSTAFF—Remaining his unique self, the knight once more demonstrates his utterly carefree attitude, his mental resiliency, his wit—and his impudence when confronted by the Chief Justice. At one point, however, Falstaff's animosity toward the latter nearly causes him to lose his usual self-confidence.

THE LORD CHIEF JUSTICE—Again he serves as severe critic of and foil to Sir John Falstaff, and as the voice of order and respectability. His character is developed somewhat in this scene, for he finds the opportunity to vie with Falstaff in punning and comes off quite well.

BARDOLPH—Falstaff's serving man.

THE PAGE—Falstaff's servant. Judging by the action in this scene and particularly by the page's two-line speech, there is no question of his loyalty to his master.

CHARACTERS NOT PRESENT BUT MENTIONED

HARRY, PRINCE OF WALES—Prince Hal, upon whose tolerance and good favor Falstaff depends.

MY LORD OF LANCASTER—John, Duke of Lancaster, brother to Prince Hal and leader of royalist troops.

THE ARCHBISHOP—Richard Scroop of York, leader of the Yorkshire rebels.

NORTHUMBERLAND—Henry Percy the elder, Earl of Northumberland and leader of northern rebels in his bailiwick.

PURPOSE OF THE SCENE

1. To give further insight into the character of Falstaff, whose disregard of law and order is emphasized by his cavalier attitude toward the Lord Chief Justice.

2. To introduce the Hostess of the Boar's-Head Tavern in person.

3. To prepare the way for the re-appearance of Prince Hal.

4. To add expository details relating to the action against the insurgents and in this way to keep to the fore the theme of rebellion.

SUGGESTED QUESTIONS

1. Why is Falstaff especially interested in learning whether or not the King plans to return soon to London?

2. What do you find revealing in the fact that Falstaff twice invites Gower to dine with him?

3. Are there any details to support Falstaff's contention that Mistress Quickly was indeed quite prosperous at one time?

ACT II — SCENE 2

SYNOPSIS

Prince Hal and Poins appear on a London street and engage in an exchange characterized by light, brilliant wit. In the amusing backchat between the two, it is made clear that Hal, very much aware of what he is doing and what the public reaction will be, chooses again to seek out the company of regulars at the Boar's-Head Tavern.

Ironically, the Prince remarks that he should not be sad because the King, his father, is sick. And cynically Poins replies that Hal's grief can not be very deep. Still good humoredly, Hal protests that his reactions to such circumstances are not to be confused with those of Falstaff or of Poins. He adds that his heart bleeds inwardly, despite the fact that, in such "vile company," he makes no outward show of grief. Poins flatly states that tears would be a sign of hypocrisy in one who associates with Falstaff. The Prince reminds him that he is no less guilty of association with Poins, and the latter makes a defense of his character just as Bardolph and the page enter.

The Prince greets Falstaff's serving man as "noble Bardolph" and remarks that the page has been transformed into an ape. Again Bardolph's "malmesey nose" becomes the source of comedy. The page declares that, seen through the red lattice windows of the tavern, Bardolph's face was indiscernible. A scurrilous interchange follows, and the Prince, amused by the page's wit, gives him a crown, to which sum Poins adds sixpence.

When the Prince inquires about Falstaff, Bardolph hands over a letter addressed to Hal. Both the Prince and Poins have a choice selection of epithets for and comments on Sir John as they peruse it. Beginning in an excessively formal manner, Falstaff has written a warning to Hal. Poins, he insists, boasts that his sister Nell is betrothed to the Prince. He then urges Hal to report "at idle times," and adds a self-laudatory close to the letter. The incensed Poins vows that he will soak the letter in sack and force Falstaff to eat it.

"Well, thus we play the fools with the time, and the spirits of the wise sit in the clouds and mock us," the Prince concludes.

Hal learns that Falstaff is at the Boar's-Head Tavern in company with the old group as well as Mistress Quickly and Doll Tearsheet. About the latter's unsavory character neither Hal nor Poins is in any doubt. The two agree to "steal upon them," and Bardolph is warned not to give advance notice that the Prince is now in London.

Alone, the Prince and Poins discuss how they can arrange to eavesdrop on Sir John without being discovered. The ingenious Poins has the answer: they will disguise themselves as lowly drawers in the tavern.

CHARACTERS IN SCENE 2

PRINCE HENRY—Hal, the heir-apparent, who again chooses to tolerate the unrestrained behavior of Falstaff and his cronies. Despite his keen wit and apparently devil-may-care manner, he is not without deep concern for his royal father nor unperturbed about affairs in the realm. Consistent with his character as drawn in *Henry IV, Part I*, he appears as a man of "all humors that have showed themselves humors since the old days of Goodman Adam." (See II. iv. 104 in the earlier play).

POINS—Hal's companion at the Boar's-Head, who delights no less than does the Prince in trapping Falstaff. It will be remembered that it was he who proposed to trick the fat knight in connection with the Gadshill robbery. In view of the accusation made in Falstaff's letter, Poins now has special reason for baiting Sir John.

BARDOLPH—Falstaff's serving man.

THE PAGE—Falstaff's little servant, now decked out in new livery.

CHARACTERS NOT PRESENT BUT MENTIONED

HAL'S FATHER—King Henry IV, who is now gravely ill at this time of national emergency.

MISTRESS QUICKLY—Hostess of the Boar's-Head Tavern.

DOLL TEARSHEET—Prostitute at the Boar's-Head Tavern.

PURPOSE OF SCENE 2

1. To re-introduce Prince Hal and Poins, filling in the outlines of character, particularly that of the former.
2. To start the action involving comic conflict between Hal and Falstaff.
3. To provide expository details regarding the King's health.

SUGGESTED QUESTIONS

1. Why does Poins believe that Hal cannot be deeply worried about the King's health?
2. What possibly could be the motivation for Falstaff's libel of Poins?
3. What does Prince Hal mean when he says to Poins, "Never a man's thought in the world keeps the roadway better than thine" (lines 62-63)?

ACT II – SCENE 3

Before Warkworth Castle the Earl of Northumberland, Lady Northumberland and Lady Percy seriously discuss the Earl's plans. The two ladies vehemently urge Northumberland to avoid participation in the rising against Henry IV, but he replies that his honor is at stake since he has given his word to join the insurgents. Lady Percy reminds him that honor had not prevented him from failing to appear at Shrewsbury when Hotspur sorely needed his father's help. Describing her late husband as the "miracle of men," she bitterly argues that with half the number now led by the Archbishop and the Lord Marshal (Mowbray), he would have defeated the royalists and have survived.

Lady Northumberland urges her husband to hurry to Scotland and to remain there until he learned how the insurgents fared in battle. At first unable to make up his mind, the Earl then agrees to follow her counsel.

CHARACTERS IN SCENE 3

NORTHUMBERLAND—Henry Percy the elder, Earl of Northumberland. His decision to leave for Scotland after having given his word to lead his forces in support of those raised by the

Archbishop of York points to the conclusion that the same concern for his own safety explains his failure to appear at Shrewsbury, where Hotspur, his son, faced the royal forces.

LADY NORTHUMBERLAND—Wife of the Earl and mother of the slain Hotspur, understandably concerned for the safety of her husband.

LADY PERCY—Katherine (Kate), sister of Edmund Mortimer, Earl of March, and widow of Hotspur. Her deep love for her dead husband, well established in the earlier play, is underscored in this scene.

CHARACTERS NOT PRESENT BUT MENTIONED

THE ARCHBISHOP—Richard Scroop, Archbishop of York, active critic of Henry IV.

THE MARSHAL—Thomas, second Duke of Norfolk and Earl Marshal of England, now allied with the rebellious Archbishop.

HOTSPUR—Henry Percy, son of the Earl of Northumberland, slain by Prince Hal at Shrewsbury.

MONMOUTH—Prince Hal (Henry of Monmouth).

PURPOSE OF THE SCENE

1. To advance the main plot, making clear the fact that the numerically inferior troops led by John of Lancaster at least will not have to deal with forces mustered by Northumberland.

2. To provide another link between the first and second parts of *Henry IV* by reference to Hotspur and to events dramatized in the earlier play.

SUGGESTED QUESTIONS

1. What is meant by Northumberland's phrase "visage of the times" (line 3)?

2. How may one paraphrase "nothing but the sound of Hotspur's name/ Did seem defensible"?

3. Aside from his promises, why is the Earl at first convinced that he must join forces with the Archbishop?

ACT II – SCENE 4

SYNOPSIS

From the conversation of two lowly drawers at the Boar's-Head Tavern, the audience learns of another way in which Prince Hal had baited Falstaff by giving him five apples with wrinkled skins and identifying the knight as the sixth. They further learn that, at Doll Tearsheet's request, musicians have been sent for, and that the Prince and Poins will soon appear and borrow the drawer's jerkins and aprons.

The Hostess and Doll Tearsheet enter, the former complimenting Doll on her improved health—that is, on having recovered from the excessive drinking of wine. Next, Falstaff makes his appearance singing a ballad. He is solicitous about Doll's health, and the two engage in their respective types of badinage, often a bit scandalous. The Hostess is an appreciative audience, and her comments admit to interpretation at two levels, one inadvertently uncomplimentary to both parties. At the end of this verbal exchange, Doll remarks that she will remain friends with Falstaff since he is going to the wars.

The First Drawer announces the arrival of Pistol, who wants a word with Falstaff. At the mention of Pistol's name, Doll vociferously denounces him as a "swaggering rascal" and a "foul-mouthed rogue." The Hostess, once more striving to keep up the appearance of respectability, vows that no swaggerers are welcome in her establishment. Falstaff then identifies Pistol as his "ancient" (a standard-bearer for a leader of troops) and states that he is a "tame-cheater" (confidence man) who is as gentle as a puppy. After the Hostess engages in another exercise in the misuse of words, Pistol is called for. He enters with Bardolph and the page.

Falstaff invites Pistol to drink a toast first to the Hostess and then to Doll. But the latter will have none of it. She and the ancient have a virulent interchange, Doll excoriating Pistol and Pistol making blood-curdling threats to avenge himself. It remains a question who is the more devastating—the billingsgate which pours from the lips of Doll or the ranting of Pistol.

The disguised Prince Hal and Poins now follow the musicians into the room. Completely unaware of their presence, Falstaff talks freely and most indiscreetly to Doll Tearsheet, who is seated on his lap. He blandly informs her that the Prince is a shallow fellow fit only to be a pantryman, and that Poins ("that baboon") is tolerated only because he is young and wild like the Prince. Hal and Poins exchange witty and appropriate remarks on the slander and on Falstaff's behavior with Doll Tearsheet.

At last Falstaff notices the two drawers and makes unflattering remarks on their resemblance to the Prince and to Poins. Hal's denunciation of the fat knight gives the show away, and the Hostess welcomes Hal, as does Falstaff in his own brash style. But Doll, who had lauded Falstaff as a valorous man, now denounces him as a coward for permitting Hal to insult him.

Poins warns the Prince that Falstaff will surely extricate himself from his predicament if there is any delay in attack. Flatly stating that he had overheard every word, Hal ironically adds that plump Jack, no doubt, will revive the specious argument he had used after running away at Gadshill and claim that he was aware of Hal's presence all along. But the knight, well aware that such a story will not serve him now, calmly admits that he did not recognize the Prince. He has a new, original defense: so far from abusing the Prince he had sought to defend him from the wicked. If he, Falstaff, had voiced praise, they would have fallen in love with the heir-apparent. Hal seizes upon the word "wicked." Who are these "wicked" Falstaff speaks of? Surely not this "virtuous woman," Doll Tearsheet; surely not the Hostess! Did the knight then mean Bardolph, "whose zeal burns in his nose"? Or the page, perhaps?

Falstaff's wit does not desert him. He argues that all named are, in one way or another, wicked—even the little page, despite the "good angel about him." The Hostess, once more sensitive about her reputation, protests; and the two engage in an amusing colloquy.

Peto enters with important news. The King is at Westminster, and messengers have arrived from the North. Moreover, no less than a dozen captains have been asking for Falstaff. Prince Hal reproves himself for wasting time, calls for his sword and cloak, and bids Sir John goodnight. Poins, Peto, and Bardolph leave with him.

Bardolph returns immediately with the news that the captains are waiting at the door for Falstaff, who must leave at once for Court. Sir John says his farewells to the Hostess and Doll Tearsheet, urging them to note "how men of merit are sought after." Both women are distraught as he leaves. But a moment later they hear Bardolph call from another room: "Bid Mistress Tearsheet come to my master." "Oh, run, Doll, run," blubbers the Hostess.

CHARACTERS IN SCENE 4

FALSTAFF—For the first time in *Henry IV, Part I*, the audience views Sir John at his calling in the Boar's-Head Tavern, where he reigns supreme. He is revealed as one devoted to the pleasures of the flesh and as a gargantuan liar — but also as one who is indeed not only witty in himself but the cause of wit in other men. It is to be noted that, however much he has taken advantage of the Hostess and used Doll Tearsheet, both are devoted to him.

PISTOL — For the first time the audience meets one of Shakespeare's "humors" characters, a man who is comically unbalanced in a particular way. Pistol's humor is that he poses as a man who is a ferocious warrior, laconic but startling in speech. Shakespeare uses him partly to burlesque characters in plays notable for bombast which had wide popular appeal. Close students of Elizabethan drama recognize many verbal echoes in Pistol's lines. For example, when he speaks of the "pampered jades of Asia," he borrows a phrase from Christopher Marlowe's *Tamberlaine, Part II*. There are several more inferior plays presented by a rival company. Actually this "fustian rascal" is a poltroon, an arrant coward. Thus Shakespeare makes the most of comic incongruity.

MISTRESS QUICKLY — The kindly, if weak, owner of the Boar's Head Tavern — still the mistress not only of the tavern but of malapropisms.

DOLL TEARSHEET — A prostitute who is "as common as the way between St. Albans and London," to borrow Poins' words (II.ii.184-185), she is a spirited character who is never at loss for words, usually invectives. If her charms are usually for hire, she nevertheless reserves a special place for Falstaff in her affections.

PRINCE HAL — At the comic level, the Prince who had vindicated his honor at Shrewsbury, once again crosses swords with Falstaff. Perhaps some will call the encounter a draw. But one should observe how Hal urbanely controls himself and, once more endorsing the precept that life should have its lighter moments, joins with Poins in gulling Sir John.

POINS — The ingenious baiter of Falstaff and therefore welcome as Hal's associate in the comic subplot.

PETO — One of Falstaff's companions.

BARDOLPH — Falstaff's serving man.

THE PAGE — Falstaff's serving boy.

PURPOSE OF THE SCENE

1. To present the initial encounter between Falstaff and Prince Hal, one which balances the Gadshill episode in *Henry IV, Part I*.

2. To advance the action of the comic subplot and at the same time not to lose sight of the theme of rebellion.

3. To develop the characters of the newly created Doll Tearsheet and Pistol.

4. To add to the characterization of Prince Hal and Mistress Quickly.

SUGGESTED QUESTIONS

1. Doll Tearsheet praises Falstaff as "valorous as Hector of Troy, worth five Agammemnons, and ten times better than the Nine Worthies" (lines 236-238). How may one explain these allusions?

2. What does Doll Tearsheet mean when she denounces Pistol as a "fustian rascal"?

3. How well does Falstaff come off in this scene as compared to the one following the Gadshill robbery in *Henry IV, Part I*?

A C T   I I I – S C E N E   1

SYNOPSIS

It is past midnight. Henry IV, now at the Palace in Westminster, instructs a page to call in the Earls of Warwick and Surrey to consider the import of the news received from the north. Ailing and exhausted, the King invokes sleep and laments the fact that its soothing balm, freely enjoyed by the lowliest of subjects, is denied him: "Uneasy lies the head that wears a crown."

The two earls enter and, in reply to the King's question, state that they have studied the letters and are aware of the "rank disease" which now infects the realm. Warwick reassures the worried Henry, arguing that good advice and little medicine will effect a cure – that is, Northumberland (whose decision to fly to Scotland they know nothing about) will be subdued. Henry exclaims that, if one could see into the future and become aware of the perils which await, not even the happiest youth would choose to live. These thoughts lead him to recall earlier events relating to Richard II, Northumberland, and himself, most of which were dramatized in Shakespeare's earlier chronicle history, *Richard II*. He speaks of how Northumberland, once loyal to Richard, had joined forces with Henry himself against the reigning monarch. Especially Henry recalls Richard's ominous prophecy that the day would come when Northumberland would turn traitor again. Warwick discounts the possibility of there being anything supernatural in Richard's prophecy. The King replies that, since such events seem to be un-avoidable, they must be accepted. But he remains deeply troubled, for he has heard that the northern rebels now have a force of 50,000 men. Again Warwick reassures him. The report is rumour which always exaggerates. He expresses confidence that the royal army now in the field will defeat the insurgents. And he has one piece of good news: Glendower is dead. Warwick then urges the King to rest. Henry accepts this counsel and declares that, once order is restored, he and his lieutenants will leave for the Holy Land.

CHARACTERS IN SCENE 1

HENRY IV—The ailing King of England, exhausted by loss of sleep and beset by worries. As was true in the earlier play, Shakespeare presents him as a ruler who, determined and capable though he is, suffers the "unquiet mind" of one who is guilty of usurpation and regicide. It is necessary for one to recognize the two-fold point of view here. Henry *is* a sinner, and that he should endure rebellion is part of his punishment; yet he wears the crown on God's sufferance. Those who rebel against him are in turn grie-vous sinners who have invited God's vengeance.

WARWICK—Richard de Beauchamp, Earl of Warwick, a man famous as a brave and chivalrous warrior who had fought against the King's enemies in the Welsh wars and at Shrewsbury. In this scene he is erroneously referred to as Neville.

SURREY—Thomas FitzAlan, Earl of Arundel and Earl of Surrey. Since his father had been beheaded for treason during the reign of Richard II, his adherence to the Lancastrian cause is read-ily understood.

CHARACTERS NOT PRESENT BUT MENTIONED

THE EARL OF NORTHUMBERLAND—"This Percy," chief of the baronial family now opposed to the man they had helped to put on the throne.

THE BISHOP—The Archbishop of York, active leader of the rebel force now assembled in Yorkshire.

GLENDOWER—Leader of Welsh forces opposing the King.

PURPOSE OF THE SCENE

1. To introduce the King personally and to show how he suffers from the problems of conscience and kingship.

2. To review some of the events dramatized in *Henry IV, Part I.*

3. To emphasize the elements of conflict in the main plot, notably those relating to the grave dangers which threaten Henry's government.

SUGGESTED QUESTIONS

1. What evidence is there of an adverse turn in the fortunes of the northern insurgents?

2. Why does the King hope to go to the Holy Land?

3. What is meant by "partial sleep" (line 26)?

ACT III – SCENE 2

SYNOPSIS

Before his home in Gloucestershire, Shallow greets Silent, his fellow justice and kinsman. He inquires about the health of Silent's wife and daughter, and about the progress of son William, a student at Oxford. William, he says, must go on to the Inns of Court, the law schools in London. Shallow himself had attended Clement's Inn, and he is confident that his reputation as a wild young fellow still survives there. Among the roisterers whom he recalls is Sir John Falstaff, whom he identifies as one-time page to Thomas Mowbray, Duke of Norfolk. It is this same knight who will arrive soon to obtain recruits, so Shallow informs Silent. And he rambles on, commenting on Falstaff's prowess in brawling when both were young. He continues to talk now of the inevitability of death, now of the price of livestock.

Bardolph and another of Falstaff's men enter. When Shallow identifies himself, Corporal Bardolph (such is his new military title) conveys his master's greeting. The delighted justice lauds Falstaff as an expert with the backsword and inquires about the knight's health and that of "his lady his wife." Bardolph replies that a soldier is better accommodated than with a wife. Shallow is enchanted by the expression "better accommodated." Respectfully, the Corporal points out that it is not a phrase but a word—a soldier-like word.

And he defines it in terms of itself. Accommodated, it seems, means accommodated.

Falstaff enters and is effusively welcomed. When Shallow introduces him to Justice Silent, the knight remarks that a man with such a name is well fitted to administer the law. Then to business. Shallow assures Sir John that he has a dozen fit men among whom good recruits may be found. Four are successively called to be questioned, and the name of each gives Falstaff wonderful opportunity to display his wit.

The first is Ralph Mouldy, described as "a good-limbed fellow, young and strong and of good family." Falstaff remarks that Mouldy should indeed be put to use. Shallow, anxious to prove that he is not obtuse, explains the joke — "things mouldy lack use." Despite Mouldy's protests that his wife will object, he is chosen as the first recruit.

Next is Simon Shadow, who helpfully identifies himself as his mother's son, giving Falstaff the chance to make the inevitable conclusion that Shadow is the natural son of some unknown male. Sir John approves of the name, however, for he needs man "shadows" to complete his roster. So Simon becomes the second recruit.

Thomas Wart, the third to be considered, does not pass muster; he is far too ragged — a "very ragged wart," indeed.

Francis Feeble next steps forth and is identified as a woman's tailor. Falstaff ironically observes that he will be "as valiant as the wrathful dove or most magnanimous mouse." He is accepted as the third recruit.

Then comes Peter Bullcalf, protesting that he is a "diseased" man. But his explanation that he had caught cold while ringing bells on Coronation Day does not help him. Falstaff curtly states that Peter will "go to the wars in a gown" — that is, whether he is sick or not.

Shallow interrupts to invite Sir John to dine with him, but Falstaff politely refuses, adding that he is most happy to see his old friend. With this cue, the harmlessly vain justice recalls more wild episodes in which the two had been involved during their student days. At last Silent manages to say something. He remarks that fifty-five years have passed since his kinsman was at Clement's Inn. Humoring Justice Shallow, Falstaff exclaims, "We have heard the chimes ring at midnight," and he leaves the stage in company of the two.

Immediately both Peter Bullcalf and Ralph Mouldy offer money to Bardolph to secure their release from duty. Peter argues that he is not concerned about himself; it is just that he does not want to go to the wars. In fact, he would rather be hanged. Ralph has a better reason. His wife is old and needs his help. Surprisingly, the "most forcible Feeble" proves to be the soul of courage. "A man can die but once," he declares, and adds that "no man's too good to serve his prince."

When Falstaff and the justices return, the knight is pleased to learn that Bardolph has had three pounds from Peter Bullcalf and Ralph Mouldy. He acts promptly. Although Shallow includes the names of these two in his list of those selected, Falstaff releases them. The perplexed justice cannot understand why, but Sir John makes everything clear: spirit, not appearance, is the test. Ragged Wart (rejected earlier), thin-faced Shadow, and Francis Feeble — they are the men for him. Ralph must be a man of spirit, since he obviously has nothing else. As for Shadow, the enemy will find him a very poor target. And Feeble, fleet of foot, will prove first-rate for retreating.

Satisfied with this explanation, Shallow once more reminisces about the good old days. Then Falstaff expresses his thanks to both justices and orders Bardolph to give coats to the new recruits. Shallow urges the knight to return and renew their old friendship, and Falstaff commands his corporal to march the men away.

In soliloquy, Falstaff makes it clear that he will indeed return to capitalize on the credulity of Shallow, whom he describes as an inveterate teller of tall tales about the past. He had remembered the justice as one who was "like a man made of cheese paring." And yet, says Falstaff to himself (and to the audience), this same Shallow is now a squire who speaks familiarly of John of Gaunt. He will prove an easy victim; Falstaff will "snap him up."

CHARACTERS IN SCENE 2

FALSTAFF — The audience now witnesses Sir John as he carries out, in his own way, initial duties as a royalist leader. It will be recalled that in *Henry IV, Part I,* he had performed the same task; but the actual recruitment was not dramatized. As he led his ragged army to Coventry, he said to Bardolph (IV.ii.12-15):

> If I be not ashamed of my soldiers, I am a soused gurnet. I have misused the King's press damnably. I have got, in exchange of a hundred and fifty soldiers, three hundred and odd pounds.

Now Shakespeare lets the audience see exactly how the artful Falstaff capitalizes on his commission to raise troops. After all, had Sir John not said that "a good wit will make use of anything?" Yet however much one may deplore Falstaff's action, he cannot avoid being vastly entertained by the wit and ingenuity. And so with the suave manner in which the knight manages his old school fellow, the gullible Justice Shallow.

JUSTICE SHALLOW — Robert Shallow, a country squire — that is, a well-born member of a prosperous county family, whose title (esquire) places him just below the rank of knight. He flourishes as justice-of-the-peace in Gloucestershire, the small county just south of Shakespeare's Warwickshire. Advanced in years, as is Falstaff himself, he lacks Sir John's incisive mind and spirit of perpetual youth. He has reached the stage where he lives much in the past, and it is his loquaciousness and uncertain re-creations of the past which result in good comedy.

JUSTICE SILENT — Shallow's admiring kinsman and fellow justice-of-the peace, whose inarticulateness provides comic contrast to the volubility of Shallow.

BARDOLPH — Falstaff's serving man, now a corporal, whose value to his master is well established in this scene.

RALPH MOULDY — The first recruit examined by Falstaff. He is identified as a member of a good, substantial family and can afford to buy his way out of service in the army.

SIMON SHADOW — The second recruit who is so thin that he is no more than a shadow of a man, and one of no family whatsoever.

THOMAS WART — The pathetically thread-bare third man to be examined by Falstaff.

FRANCIS FEEBLE — The fourth recruit, a woman's tailor, and therefore hardly a manly type. He nevertheless speaks more courageously than any of the others.

PETER BULLCALF — The bovine last recruit to be called up. His timidity provides an amusing contrast to the valor of Francis Feeble.

PURPOSE OF THE SCENE

1. To present Falstaff in his capacity as one of the King's officers exercising his commission to raise troops.

2. To introduce and develop two new, original comic characters, Shallow and Silent.

3. To prepare for one of Falstaff's later escapades which will be carried out at the expense of Justice Shallow.

4. To satirize actual malpractice relating to the recruiting of soldiers in Elizabethan England.

SUGGESTED QUESTIONS

1. What is revealing in the fact that Sir John Falstaff had been a page in the household of the Duke of Norfolk?

2. What is the point of Falstaff's remark on Silent's name: ". . . it well befits you should be of the peace"?

3. Aside from his youth and good physical condition, why should Falstaff be especially pleased to have Ralph Mouldy presented as a recruit?

4. What does Falstaff mean when he says ". . . we have a number of shadows to fill up the muster book" (lines 145-146)?

ACT IV — SCENE 1

SYNOPSIS

At Gaultree Forest in Yorkshire, the rebel leaders await the return of scouts who have been sent out to ascertain the size of the royal forces led by Prince John of Lancaster. The Archbishop of York tells his lieutenants, Mowbray and Hastings chief among them, that he has received more news from Northumberland. The Earl has written that, since he has been unable to raise a large force as befits his rank, he has retired to Scotland to wait until times are more favorable. He has only good wishes to offer the rebel leaders.

A messenger then reports that the royalists, in good formation and 30,000 strong, are no more than a mile to the West. Mowbray, noting that the insurgent's own estimate of size has thus been confirmed, is anxious to meet the enemy at once.

The Earl of Westmoreland enters. He brings greetings from his "general the Prince, Lord John and Duke of Lancaster," and a message for the Archbishop. But first he has words of reproach for the latter: why has the "Reverend Father," a man of position, learning, age, turned rebel? The Archbishop concisely states his case. Using the metaphor of "disease," he indicts the rule of Henry IV and argues that the same affliction had fatally infected the deposed and now dead Richard II. He further argues that, so far from being an enemy of peace, he is one that seeks redress of grievous wrongs. He complains that, although articles of grievance had been offered to the King, false counsellors had seen to it that no audience had been granted.

When, asks Westmoreland, had the appeal been denied? Who had stood in the Archbishop's way? In a word, he argues that there is no valid reason for such a gross misuse of high ecclesiastical office. The Archbishop then charges that Henry IV had been responsible for the death of his brother. But the Prince's emissary insists that Scroop has no need for personal redress. Mowbray breaks in to say that *all* need redress of grievances. Westmoreland goes as far as to concede that, in view of the general lawlessness, some injustices may have been inevitable. But he denies that the King is to be held responsible. He goes on to point out that the title and the estates of Mowbray's father (Duke of Norfolk) had been restored. The mention of his father's name leads Mowbray to recall the quarrel between the late Duke and Bolingbroke, now Henry IV, which had led to the banishment of both parties. He insists that, had Richard II permitted them to settle their differences in the lists of Coventry, Richard would not have lost his crown and life. But Westmoreland will have none of this. According to him, if the late Duke of Norfolk had defeated Henry in single combat, he would not have lived to leave Coventry, so great was public opinion aligned against him and in favor of Henry. All this, he adds, is mere digression. He has come to learn exactly what are the complaints of the rebels and to inform them that Prince John not only will give them audience, but, if the demands are just, great prompt redress.

Mowbray voices the first of his suspicions, arguing that this offer may be a trick. Westmoreland insists that it is an honest one, the motive for which is mercy, not fear. The royal army, confident and strong, he states, is better led than is that of the rebel leaders. In reply to a question by Lord Hastings, he assures them that, as the King's general, Prince John has full authority to act in this serious matter.

Having listened to arguments on both sides, the Archbishop requests Westmoreland to take the articles of grievance to the Prince. He promises that, if each is satisfactorily settled, the insurgents will disband. Westmoreland agrees to do so, and says that the decision will be made while both armies await within eyesight.

Again Mowbray objects. He is sure that the King will not forget their action against him and will find an excuse to punish them. But the Archbishop shares Hastings' optimism. He believes that Henry is tired of "petty" grievances and has learned that the death of one traitor leads to the birth of two others. Moreover, he argues, Henry is well aware that those who oppose him are closely allied to his friends; he dares not offend the latter. Hastings adds that, having had to commit forces elsewhere in the kingdom, Henry is now a "fangless lion." Further to conciliate the wary Mowbray, the Archbishop assures him that, if the peace does not endure, the rebel power will be all the greater.

So when Westmoreland returns with the information that John of Lancaster will meet the insurgent leaders at a place equidistant between the two armed camps, the Archbishop and his lieutenants leave promptly. "My lord, we come," are the Archbishop's final words.

CHARACTERS IN SCENE 1

THE ARCHBISHOP OF YORK—Richard Scroop, now full established as the leading spirit among the insurgents. It is he who had drawn up the articles of grievances; it is he who, after listening to opposing points of view, makes the command decision. His address to Westmoreland, as well as his success in raising a large army, emphasizes his status as a formidable opponent.

MOWBRAY—Thomas, second Duke of Norfolk and Earl Marshal of England, who, as in Act I, Scene 3, remains the cautious, skeptical leader among the rebels. But if he is dubious as regards human motives and performance, he remains confident that the rebels can defeat the royal forces.

HASTINGS—Edward, Lord Hastings, whose optimism regarding the possibility of a bloodless settlement of issues approaches wishful thinking. He serves as a foil to Mowbray in the debate at Gaultree Forest.

WESTMORELAND—Richard Neville, Earl of Westmoreland, second in command to Prince John. Here he functions as the Prince's emissary, just as Sir Walter Blunt had done for the King prior to the Battle of Shrewsbury. Like Sir Walter, he is the voice of political orthodoxy, summing up the royalist arguments against the rebel leaders.

CHARACTERS NOT PRESENT BUT MENTIONED

HENRY BOLINGBROKE AND THE EARL OF HEREFORD—The name and title of Henry IV prior to his coronation.

PRINCE JOHN—John of Lancaster, third son of Henry IV and leader of the royal army. He is referred to also as "our Princely General" and as "Lord John and Duke of Lancaster."

THE KING (referred to by Mowbray in his address to Westmoreland)—Richard II.

PURPOSE OF THE SCENE

1. To advance the action in the mainplot, bringing the major issues to a head and pointing to the possibility of an amicable settlement.

2. To clarify the respective arguments of the insurgents and of the royalists.

3. To provide a review of antecedent action, going back to the quarrel between the first Duke of Norfolk and Henry Bolingbroke, the man who now rules England.

SUGGESTED QUESTIONS

1. Why is the Archbishop convinced that Prince John will honor the conditions of peace demanded by the rebels?

2. Why is Mowbray convinced that the rebels will not be safe under any conditions?

3. What is meant by "well-appointed" in the Archbishop's reference to the newly arrived Westmoreland (line 25)?

A C T   I V – S C E N E   2

SYNOPSIS

Prince John of Lancaster courteously greets Mowbray, the Archbishop, and Hastings as the three arrive for the parley arranged by Westmoreland. As his emissary had done in the previous scene, the Prince deplores the fact that chief among the enemies of the Crown is the Archbishop of York, who appears not in the vestments of his religious calling nor in the act of explaining God's Word to his flock, but in armor and in the act of "turning the word to sword and life to death." The Archbishop concedes that he now appears in an unnatural form, but insists that he is not the King's enemy. He repeats his earlier argument: the articles of grievance which he had sent to the Court never received consideration; if those "most just and right desires" are honored, the insurgents will prove their loyalty to the King. Mowbray interposes the statement that, if the wrongs are not righted, the rebels stand ready to fight to the last man. Hastings adds that they have reinforcements to back up their demands and warns that, if the parley fails, members of their families will take up the quarrel. Prince John expresses doubt that Hastings possesses the wisdom and power to see into the future, and then, at Westmoreland's suggestion, gives his decision regarding the articles of grievance. He states that he is well pleased with them and insists that his father is not to blame for any injustice: the royal intentions have been misunderstood and some officials misused his authority. The Prince vows that "these griefs shall be with speed redressed." If the rebel leaders accept his assurance, he continues, "let the armies be disbanded at once and peace and friendship restored."

The Archbishop is quick to take John of Lancaster at his word, and Hastings promptly orders a captain to report the news to the rebel troops: "Let them have pay, and part." The leaders of the opposing factions now exchange courtesies. When shouts from the jubilant rebel forces are heard, Mowbray states that the sound would have been pleasing if it had signaled a victory.

The Prince orders Westmoreland to see to it that the royal troops are disbanded and then asks that the rebels pass in review before their dismissal. Hastings leaves to make the arrangements for carrying out the request. Westmoreland reappears and reports that, since the men had been ordered by the Prince to stand fast, they will not leave until they receive direct orders from him. "They know their orders," says the Prince significantly.

When Hastings returns with the news that the men had lost no time in leaving for their homes and places of amusement, Westmoreland immediately declares that Hastings, Mowbray, and the Archbishop are under arrest for treason. Orders are also given for the apprehension of any stragglers among the dispersed rebel forces. Protests regarding justice and honor and good faith are of no avail. The Prince bluntly tells them that he had pledged no more than a redress of grievances—a pledge which he will keep. As for the three leaders, he concludes, let them expect to receive the punishment which awaits all traitors. "God, not we, hath safely fought today," he adds as he orders the traitors to be brought to the "block of death."

CHARACTERS IN SCENE 2

PRINCE JOHN OF LANCASTER — Third son of Henry IV and general of the royal forces. He appears here as a Machiavellian figure, one who will use any means to achieve his purpose. As was stated in the introduction above, his apparent perfidy seems inexcusable to modern audiences. To them he emerges as a hypocrite. Certainly it would be more pleasing to see him manifest the chivalry and courage which marked his older brother's conduct at

36

Shrewsbury. It may be argued that Shakespeare was restricted by his source or sources, that he could not take gross liberty with history known to all literate members of his audience. Or it may be argued that, had John of Lancaster won a victory in honorable combat, he may well have emerged as the hero of the play. Finally, the historical approach must not be ignored in passing judgment on Prince John. According to orthodox Tudor political theory, which informs the chronicle history plays by Shakespeare and which was to a large extent based upon the Scriptures, the King was indeed God's deputy on earth—God's "substitute," as the Prince calls him (line 28). No subject for any reason had the right actively to oppose him. Just such promises as those made by the Prince were made to the rebels against Henry VIII in 1536. When the insurgent leaders accepted the King's promises for a redress of grievances and dismissed their followers, Henry VIII's officers arrested them as traitors, and they went to their deaths. At that time the question of perfidy was not even raised. Shakespeare's audiences, we may assume, were not offended by Prince John's action.

THE EARL OF WESTMORELAND—Ralph Neville, second-in-command of the royal troops and dependable instruments of Prince John's strategy.

THE ARCHBISHOP OF YORK—Richard Scroop, the courageous spirit of the northern insurgents, but a leader who is proved to be tragically gullible.

HASTINGS—Edward, Lord Hastings, who is the complete optimist, believing that the rebels will win a bloodless victory.

MOWBRAY—Thomas, second Duke of Norfolk, the realist among the rebel leaders, whose misgivings early and late regarding the intent of the royalists mark him as a man of keen insight.

CHARACTER NOT PRESENT BUT MENTIONED

THE KING—Henry IV, who, according to Prince John, is not to be held responsible for any injustices against his subjects.

PURPOSE OF THE SCENE

1. To provide the resolution to the main action as regards the dominant theme of rebellion.
2. To fill in the outlines of Prince John's character, actually in contrast to that of the heir apparent, Prince Hal. Prince John is depicted as a cold politician, a man who lacks the breadth and charm

of his older brother.

    3. From a doctrinal point of view, to show that "Thus ever did rebellion find rebuke."

SUGGESTED QUESTIONS

    1. How do you explain the metaphor used by the Archbishop when he refers to "this Hydra son of war" (line 38)?

    2. What does Mowbray mean when, in reply to Westmoreland's toast, he makes the following comment (lines 79-80)?

You wish me health in very happy season,
For I am, on sudden, something ill.

ACT IV – SCENE 3

SYNOPSIS

    Noise of armed conflict is heard as Falstaff and a stranger enter. In response to questioning, the latter identifies himself as Colevile of the Dale, a knight. Falstaff charges him with being a traitor who belongs in a dungeon. Asked if this is not Sir John Falstaff who addresses him, the fat knight goes no further than to say that he is as good a man; and he demands that Colevile surrender rather than suffer "fear and trembling." Colevile, convinced that this is Sir John, agrees to submit. His captor then reflects on the fact that his enormous girth always reveals his identity.

    Prince John of Lancaster, the Earl of Westmoreland, and one Blunt arrive. The Prince orders the Earl to assemble the troops since the fighting is over, and then asks Falstaff where he had been, pointedly making reference to the knight's "tardy tricks" — his gift for turning up only when the danger is over. Falstaff is injured innocence personified. Heretofore, he states, he had not known that rebuke and check were the rewards for valor. He insists that he had exhausted many post horses in his dash to the battlefield. Now he is here, "in . . . pure and immaculate valor," the captor of a dangerous enemy. Comparing himself to Caesar, Falstaff concludes that he came, he saw, he conquered. But the Prince is sure that Colevile's courtesy, not Sir John's bravery, explains the capture. Falstaff remains Falstaff. As he turns Colevile over to the Prince, he demands that his valor be celebrated in a broadside ballad illustrated with a picture of Colevile kissing Falstaff's foot. Then he will be sure to get true credit, outshining all others. There follows a brief colloquy between the Prince and Colevile, who conducts himself with courage and dignity. Falstaff interrupts on three occasions, anxious to make good his latest fabrication.

Westmoreland returns to report that the Prince's orders have been carried out and the royal forces are now re-assembling. The Prince then orders his men to take Colevile and all other captives to York for immediate execution. Joined by his chief lieutenants, he himself will leave for Court, where his father lies ill. Falstaff asks permission to return by way of Gloucestershire and urges the Prince to report him favorably at Court. Bidding him farewell, John of Lancaster says that he will speak better of Falstaff than the knight deserves.

Alone, Falstaff soliloquizes. He is aware that Prince John has little use for him. And little wonder. This "sober-blooded boy" drinks no wine; all such abstainers are notorious weaklings – and usually fools and cowards. Falstaff then expounds the virtues he finds in sherris sack. According to him, it enters the brain, making a man lively, inventive, witty; it warms the blood, giving him courage; it illumines the face, which then serves as a beacon warning the whole man to arm himself. And this moves the heart to direct the performance of valorous deeds. Thus it is, Falstaff continues, that Prince Henry is valiant. Like Prince John, he had interited cold blood from his father, but good wine had transformed him. If Falstaff had one thousand sons, each would be taught the virtues of sack.

Bardolph enters and tells his master that all the soldiers have been discharged and dispersed. In effect, the knight says, "Good riddance." As for him, he will waste no time in seeking out Master Robert Shallow, whom he has already softened up for his purpose.

CHARACTERS IN SCENE 3

SIR JOHN FALSTAFF – Once more on the battlefield, Falstaff is presented in this scene which balances the one in *Henry IV, Part I,* wherein he claimed to have slain Hotspur. So well individualized is the knight that it would be misleading to reduce him to a type character. Nevertheless, one aspect of his complex character is that of the Braggart Warrior, a favorite in comedy dating back to Roman comedy and taken over into popular drama of Western Europe during the Renaissance. Some among Falstaff's admirers will argue that he does not expect to be believed, so patently false are his claims; and from that point of view is not a liar at all. At least one thing is indisputable, however: Falstaff again proves that "a good wit will make use of anything." His soliloquy on the virtues of sack is a justly famous bravura piece, completely in character.

SIR JOHN COLEVILE OF THE DALE — A representative of the upper class in northern England, many members of which answered the Archbishop of York's call to arms. His obvious good breeding and courage invite the sympathy of the audience.

PRINCE JOHN OF LANCASTER — However one may judge the Prince as a result of the ruse which led to the collapse of the revolt, it must be recognized that he is a firm, competent leader who moves relentlessly against enemies of the Crown. Aware of Falstaff's tricks, he does not hesitate to reprove the knight, but does not deign to engage in argument or railery with him.

WESTMORELAND — Ralph Neville, Earl of Westmoreland, who continues to function as the Prince's dependable right-hand man.

BARDOLPH — Falstaff's serving man.

CHARACTER NOT PRESENT BUT MENTIONED

MASTER ROBERT SHALLOW, ESQUIRE — The justice-of-the-peace in Gloucestershire who assisted Falstaff in the recruitment of troops.

PURPOSE OF THE SCENE

1. To present Falstaff at his calling now in the rebellious north, showing how he executed his commission as one of the King's officers and thus to enlarge the comic characterization of the knight.

2. To provide Falstaff with the opportunity to explain once more his philosophy of life and, in the process thereof, to illuminate not only his own character but the characters of Prince Hal and Prince John as well.

3. To forge the link between main plot and comic subplot of the play.

SUGGESTED QUESTIONS

1. In what ways does Sir John Colevile of the Dale serve as a foil to Falstaff?

2. What does Falstaff exactly mean when he says, "Colevile shall still be your name..."?

3. Why does Prince John go so far as to say that he will report Falstaff better than the knight deserves?

ACT IV – SCENE 4

SYNOPSIS

King Henry IV lies ill in a room known as the Jerusalem Chamber. Two of his sons, Princes Thomas of Clarence and Humphrey of Gloucester enter with the Earl of Warwick and others. Addressing the group the King states that, if civil dissension has been surpassed and his health improves, he will lead the flower of England on a new crusade to the Holy Land. The ships and troops are ready for such an enterprise. He then asks Humphrey where Prince Henry is. The younger Prince can only reply that his elder brother may be hunting in Windsor Forest. Learning that Thomas of Clarence is present, the King then asks why he is not with his oldest brother, who always had favored Clarence. He urges him to cherish the affection so that he can help his brother when the latter assumes regal authority.

All this leads King Henry to comment on the heir-apparent's character: if Prince Hal is humored, he is gracious and kind of heart; if aroused he can be like flint. Therefore he must be carefully studied. The younger brother must reprove him when he is unduly mirthful, but must do so tactfully. In this way Clarence will prove to be a strong support to Prince Hal.

When the King learns that Hal is actually dining in the company of Poins and other lowly associates, he grieves for his son and heir, using the metaphor of "weeds" to describe those whom the Prince now seeks out. What will happen to England, he asks, if Hal's "headstrong riot has no curb?" Warwick speaks up and argues that the King misjudges his son. According to him, the Prince is schooling himself to understand even the lowliest subject. He predicts that Hal will "turn past evils to advantage." Sententiously the King expresses doubts about the probability of sudden reformation.

Westmoreland enters and is welcomed as the bearer of happy tidings. Harcourt immediately follows and reports that Northumberland and Lord Bardolph are captives of the Sheriff of Yorkshire. But such good news does not improve the health of the now physically weak King. All try to comfort him. Warwick is sure that he will soon recover. But Thomas of Clarence is more realistic. He points out that incessant care and labor have brought his father close to death. When Humphrey voices his concern about possible trouble among the King's subjects incident to the succession,

Thomas of Clarence is reminded that the river Thames had over-flowed its banks three times, just as it had done when Edward III lay at death's door. At last the King revives and asks to be removed to another chamber.

CHARACTERS IN SCENE 4

KING HENRY IV—After having heard several earlier refer-ences to the King's health, the audience now sees the ruler des-perately ill in the Jerusalem Chamber. His concern about Prince Hal emphasizes one of the important conflicts in the play.

HUMPHREY OF GLOUCESTER—Youngest son of Henry IV, who survived to become regent of England for a time after the death of Henry V.

THOMAS OF CLARENCE—Second son of Henry IV, who became the trusted lieutenant of Henry V in the French Wars.

WARWICK—Richard de Beauchamp, Earl of Warwick, fa-mous as a brave and chivalrous warrior who distinguished himself in the Welch wars and at Shrewsbury.

WESTMORELAND—Ralph Neville, Earl of Westmoreland, chief lieutenant to Prince John of Lancaster.

HARCOURT—An officer in the royal army.

CHARACTER NOT PRESENT BUT MENTIONED

PRINCE HENRY—The heir-apparent whose absence from his father's bedside makes understandable doubts about his real character. The King's words to Thomas of Clarence help to make clear the breadth and complexity of his character.

PURPOSE OF THE SCENE

1. To advance the important theme of the King's relations with his eldest son.

2. To add details concerning the character and reputation of Prince Hal and thus to prepare for the resolution of the play.

3. To provide additional exposition regarding the present state of the realm and the King's aspirations.

SUGGESTED QUESTIONS

1. What are the debits and credits in Hal's character as described by the King?

2. What does the King mean when he announces the intention of drawing "no swords but what are sanctified" (line 4)?

3. In what sense are "the old folk, time's doting chronicles" (line 126)?

ACT IV – SCENE 5

SYNOPSIS

Attending the ailing King is the same group who were present in the previous scene. Henry, oppressed by the respectful silence, asks for "some noise" and specifically for some music to minister to his weary spirit. As Warwick gives the order for music to be played in the next room, the King directs that his crown be placed on a pillow next to him.

Prince Henry enters and learns that his father is gravely ill and now disposed to sleep. All leave except the heir-apparent, who says he will keep watch at his father's bedside. Observing the crown, he philosophizes about it as a symbol of care and anxiety. On his father's lip he notices a feather which, he assumes, would not remain stationary if the King were breathing. He therefore concludes that his father has died. In soliloquy, the Prince states that he owes his father heart-felt grief and will pay the debt, and that his father owes him the imperial crown. Young Henry then lifts the crown and places it on his head, reflecting that just as he lawfully inherits it from his father, so he will pass it on to his heir and thus maintain unbroken the line of succession. He leaves the chamber through a door not leading into the one where the others await.

Suddenly awaking, the King calls for Warwick, Gloucester, and Clarence, who immediately enter. He learns that his eldest son has been in the chamber. Correctly assuming that Hal had taken the crown, he orders Warwick to find the heir-apparent and "chide him hither." To the King, his son's action is as great a cause of suffering as is the illness which has brought him close to death. He points the moral in words addressed to Gloucester and Clarence: gold leads sons to turn against fathers who have exercised every care in their training and welfare. Warwick returns to report that Prince Henry is in the next room washing tears of grief from his face. When the Prince enters, all others are asked to leave.

Prince Henry's first words are that he had not expected to see his father alive—words which the King interprets to mean that his son had hoped to find him dead. In a touching speech he reproves the Prince for being so impatient to wear the crown. Thus, says the King, the Prince has proved that he had no love for his father, and adds that unruly behavior all along had pointed to such a conclusion. He urges young Henry to dig his father's grave and order the ringing of "merry bells" announcing the crowning of a new ruler. As for himself, the King sadly concludes, let him be buried and forgotten. In despair Henry IV then predicts what he is sure will ensue: vanity and misrule will flourish; wise counsellors will be dismissed; "apes of idleness" and ruffians will flock to the court; the new ruler will give license to disorder and vice.

At last the Prince speaks. Had he not been choked by grief, he says, he would not have remained silent so long. Kneeling before the King, he declares that the crown belongs solely to his father, and he expresses the fervent hope that his father may live long to wear it. He assures the King that he respects Henry IV's honor and renown and remains his obedient subject. Prince Henry goes on to explain that he honestly believed that his father had died and that the very thought had chilled him to the heart. He insists that, if his words are false, he himself should not survive to realize his father's hope for reformation. Young Henry further explains that he had taken the crown, symbol of royal power and awful responsibility, and had upbraided it: the crown had fed upon the body of his father, and since it had "eaten the bearer up," other gold than that of the crown was to be more prized. At that moment, the Prince continues, he had placed the crown on his head—not with any thought of pride or pleasure, but as a kind of challenge to its tyrannical power. He concludes by saying that, if selfishness had motivated his action, he deserved to become like the poorest slave who kneels before the crown in awe and terror.

Obviously affected by Prince Henry's words, the King replies that God had led his son so to comfort him. He bids his son listen to his last words. Sorrowfully, the elder Henry admits that he had come to the throne "by . . . bypaths and crooked ways, as God knows," and had experienced a troublesome reign. But young Henry, he is sure, will fare better; for his son will wear a crown by right of succession. Old animosities will have died. Nevertheless, the King fears that his son will not be firm enough. He points out that, in order to forestall dissension among restive subjects, he had planned to lead a crusade to the Holy Land. The King then implores God to forgive him for deposing an anointed ruler (Richard II) and to grant that his son have a tranquil reign.

Prince Henry vows that, since his father won the crown, wore it, and gave it to him, he will defend it against all the world.

Prince John of Lancaster enters and greets his father. The King praises him for bringing "happiness and peace," but says that Prince John sees him fatally ill. Prince Henry promptly calls for Warwick, who enters with the others. When the King asks the name of the chamber where he "first did swoon," he learns that it is called Jerusalem. He recalls that, years earlier, it had been prophesied that he would die in Jerusalem, but he had assumed that the name referred to the Holy Land. Henry IV finally directs that he be carried to the chamber: "In that Jerusalem shall Harry die."

CHARACTERS IN SCENE 5

HENRY IV—Here the titular hero of the play emerges as a fully realized human being who wins the sympathy of all who behold and listen to him. He is above all the loving father, mourning because, now having reached the end of life, all the care he had bestowed upon his son and heir seems to have been wasted. Second, he is the conscience-stricken and penitent sinner, tormented by the knowledge that he had deposed an anointed ruler. He is sure that the civil dissension which characterized his reign and Prince Henry's waywardness are part of the punishment meted out by a just God. But his grief transcends the personal; he is deeply concerned for the safety and well-being of England.

PRINCE HENRY—The heir-apparent, misunderstood by his royal father as in the earlier play, finally vindicates himself in his father's eyes. If there are any doubts about the sincerity of his avowals, one should recall earlier evidence in this play pointing unmistakenly to young Henry's genuine affection and respect for his father. In this scene, Shakespeare takes special care to prepare the way for the Prince's rejection of Falstaff.

HUMPHREY OF GLOUCESTER—Youngest son of Henry IV.

THOMAS OF CLARENCE—Second son of Henry IV.

JOHN OF LANCASTER—Third son of Henry IV.

WARWICK—Richard de Beauchamp, Earl of Warwick and trusted counsellor of Henry IV.

SUGGESTED QUESTIONS

1. Aside from the reason given by Henry IV himself, why may he have been so anxious to lead a crusade to the Holy Land?
2. What examples of irony do you find in this important scene?
3. To whom and to what does the King refer in lines 205-207?

And all my friends, which thous must make
    thy friends,
Have but their stings and teeth newly ta'en out,
By whose fell working I was first advanced. . . .

A C T   V – S C E N E   1

SYNOPSIS

At his home in Gloucestershire, Master Robert Shallow insists that Sir John Falstaff remain his guest for the night and hospitably refuses to accept an excuse. He calls for Davy, one of his servants, and in his bumbling manner proceeds to give him instructions. Here the immediate source of the comic effect is incongruity and anticlimax. Orders and reports relating to preparations for dinner are mixed with those relating successively to planting wheat, a bill received from a blacksmith, the repairing of a chain for a well bucket, and fining the cook for losing sack at a local fair. Finally Davy is told that Falstaff ("the man of war") will stay all night. As the justice says, it is a good thing to have a friend at Court. Davy is instructed to treat Sir John's men well, for they are "arrant knaves" and may "back-bite." The term "back-bite" gives Davy the chance to pun on the fact that all of Falstaff's men wear soiled linen infected with vermin.

Although dismissed, Davy remains to intercede on the behalf of one William Visor, who is to appear in a law suit before the Justice. He agrees that Visor is an arrant knave (one of Shallow's favorite expressions), but argues that, in view of his eight years of service he – Davy – should be allowed to gain special consideration for a knave who is an honest friend. Shallow says that Visor will not suffer and again dismisses Davy.

After greeting Bardolph and the page, the Justice invites Falstaff to follow him. Sir John gives orders to his servants and remains alone on the stage long enough to express his thoughts on the comic appearance of Shallow and to make some unflattering comments on the character of the Justice and of those who serve him. Shallow, it is clear, is as thin as his kinsman, Silent. If Sir

John were cut into staffs he would make no less than four dozen, each the size of Shallow. And if Falstaff had a case to be tried before the foolish Justice he would go to work on the servants. He concludes with the moral reflection that all men should be careful of the company they keep if they are to avoid boorish behavior. Finally, plump Jack says that he will have enough fun at Shallow's expense to entertain Prince Hal continuously for a year. He then answers the Justice's call and leaves the stage.

CHARACTERS IN SCENE 1

ROBERT SHALLOW—The country Justice who once more provides excellent comedy of physical appearance and words. If some are inclined to feel that Falstaff is taking advantage of a well-meaning friend, it is well to note that Shallow's insistence that Sir John remain his guest is not motivated wholly by unselfishness, and that the Justice's conduct on the bench is not exactly faultless.

SIR JOHN FALSTAFF—The fat knight, in constrast to Shallow, now appears as the urbane courtier and soldier. Content for a time to observe and listen, he is a keen judge of and commentator on what he sees and hears. His comic portrait of the emaciated Shallow, his shrewd remarks on the circumvention of justice, and his anticipation of the fun to be had at Shallow's expense —all are entirely in keeping with his own character.

DAVY—Shallow's serving man who indeed has become much like his master in many ways, as Falstaff observed.

BARDOLPH—Falstaff's serving man.

THE PAGE—Falstaff's diminutive servant.

CHARACTERS NOT PRESENT BUT MENTIONED

WILLIAM—Shallow's cook.

WILLIAM VISOR OF WONCOT—One of the principals in a suit to be tried before Justice Shallow.

CLEMENT PERKS—The second principal in a suit to be tried before Justice Shallow.

PRINCE HARRY—Prince Henry, or Hal.

PURPOSE OF THE SCENE

1. To develop the comic character of Justice Shallow, particularly as it is revealed in the dialogue with Davy and in Falstaff's soliloquy.

2. To advance the comic subplot wherein Falstaff continues to be pre-eminent.

SUGGESTED QUESTIONS

1. In what ways does Dave prove to be much like his master?
2. What is ironical in Falstaff's observation that "It is certain that either wise bearing or ignorant carriage is caught, as men take diseases, one of another" (lines 83-85)?

A C T   V – S C E N E   2

SYNOPSIS

In the palace at Westminster, Warwick greets the Lord Chief Justice of England. Learning that Henry IV has died, the latter expresses the wish that he had not outlived the King, in whose service he inevitably made some enemies. Warwick, aware of what the Justice has in mind, agrees that Henry V will be strongly prejudiced against him. The Chief Justice can add only sad words of resignation to fate.

The Princes Lancaster, Clarence, and Gloucester enter with Westmoreland. Observing them, Warwick expresses regret that the new King has not the temper of even the least favored of his three brothers. If young Henry were like any one of his brothers, nobles who flourished when Henry IV was alive would not have reason to expect the worst. "Oh, God, I fear all will be overturned!" exclaims the Chief Justice.

After greetings are exchanged, Gloucester and Lancaster express sympathy for the Chief Justice. In the words of Lancaster, he stands "in coldest expectation." Clarence is sure that the Justice will now have to approve of Falstaff. The Chief Justice states that he had performed the duties of his high office honorably and impartially and that if the truth did not prevail he will join the late King in death.

Henry V enters with his attendants and is greeted by the Chief Justice. He notes the evidence of fear as well as sorrow and reassures his brothers. None, he says, should expect cruelty in his Court. His brothers properly grieve for their father as he does; but they have no other reason to be sad, for he will be both father and brother to them. Their replies are rather perfunctory ones, and Henry V is aware of their lack of confidence in him. Especially he knows that the Chief Justice expects to be castigated. To him young Henry now turns. When the Justice insists that the King has no just cause to hate him, Henry reminds him of how he, the immediate heir of England, had been rebuked and imprisoned by the Chief Justice. Can this be forgotten?

With dignity and eloquence the Chief Justice states his case. He had been the instrument of the King's justice; Prince Henry had dared to strike him in court, the "very seat of justice." If the new King wishes to reject the edicts of his father, let him have a son who will spurn the royal image in the same way. The Justice concludes by inviting Henry V to bring his charges against him.

Now Henry speaks with no less eloquence and dignity. He has only praise for the amazed legal official. He approves of every word the latter had said and bids him to continue to serve—to wield the sword of justice boldly, justly, impartially. Moreover, Henry V welcomes the wise counsel of this man whom he addresses as the "father of his youth."

Henry then assures his brothers that his wildness had died with his father—that is, as King he no longer would conduct himself in a manner which would invite censor. He points out that he had survived to prove how wrong were the doleful prophets who foresaw disorder and misrule when he came to the throne. He then gives the order for the assmebly of the high court of Parliament and announces his intentions of selecting the best counsellors. With them and the help of the Chief Justice he will provide England with a government unsurpassed for order and effectiveness. Neither Prince nor peer, he concludes, will ever have occasion to pray for a new ruler.

CHARACTERS IN SCENE 2

HENRY V—The now completely reformed Prince of the earlier scenes, who, to the surprise of all others present in this scene, is the personification of magnanimity and dedication to duty. It is to be recalled that from the very beginning of the two-part chronicle history Shakespeare prepared the way for this important scene in which the apparently wayward heir to the throne embraces order and justice.

THE LORD CHIEF JUSTICE—England's leading legal official who understandably expects to be severely reprimanded and removed from office. In his longest speech he succeeds in emphasizing his absolute dedication to royal service and order within the realm.

GLOUCESTER – Humphrey, Duke of Gloucester, youngest son of Henry IV.

CLARENCE – Thomas, Duke of Clarence, second son of Henry IV.

LAN CASTER – John, Duke of Lancaster, third son of Henry IV.

WARWICK – Richard de Beauchamp, Earl of Warwick, famous warrior and favored counsellor of Henry IV.

WESTMORELAND – Ralph Neville, Earl of Westmoreland.

CHARACTERS NOT PRESENT BUT MENTIONED

FALSTAFF – Sir John, who is identified implicitly as the symbol of wildness and disrespect for the law.

HENRY IV – The deceased father of the new King, in this scene referred to as Harry (by Henry V and by Warwick) and as His Majesty (by the Lord Chief Justice).

PURPOSE OF THE SCENE

1. To present the newly crowned Henry V as the youth who made good his promise to amaze the world by his reformation – or, better perhaps, showing himself publicly in his true colors. In this sense, he does "falsify men's hopes," to use the words he had spoken in soliloquy at the end of Act I, Scene ii, of the earlier play.

2. To provide the admirable Lord Chief Justice full opportunity to make the case for law and order in the State.

3. To complete the preparation for the rejection of Falstaff.

SUGGESTED QUESTIONS

1. What image is evoked when Henry V makes reference to the "balance and the sword" (line 103)?

2. What line or lines specifically point to the impending rejection of Falstaff?

3. In what political sense can Henry V be a father to the Princes?

ACT V – SCENE 3

SYNOPSIS

In this fine comic scene, Shallow flourishes as the always amusing yet gracious country squire conducting Silent, Falstaff, Bardolph, and the page to his apple orchard, where everyone enjoys the pleasures of merry old rural England. Despite Shallow's insistence that all is barren and beggarly, there is obviously plenty, and especially plenty of good wine, of which all partake. Justice Silent, the man who had hardly a word to say in the earlier scene, is irrepressible as he bursts forth with one drinking song after another and is completely unrestrained in his remarks. Falstaff, already well fortified with sack, commends Shallow on his hospitality and Silent on his unexpected conviviality. Davy, now the ubiquitous serving man, darts in and out, seeing to it that everyone is served. "Lack nothing. Be merry," are the words of Shallow. And indeed all have an abundance and all are merry.

Davy announces the arrival of Pistol, who has hurried from the Court with momentous news. Falstaff, instantly alert, instructs Davy to admit him at once. Pistol indeed has important intelligence, but takes his time in conveying it. Sir John, he announces, is now "one of the greatest men of the realm." Silent, now very deep in his cups, expresses the opinion that one Goodman Puff is greater. And this gives Pistol the cue to explode as he denounces the harmless Silent as a "most recreant coward base." Still ranting, he finally manages to inform Falstaff that he has "happy news of price." Sir John, adopting the bombastic style, urges him to report it. Silent revives to sing lines from a Robin Hood ballad, and Justice Shallow interrupts to adjudicate. He says that there are two courses to follow —either reveal the news or conceal it. And he adds that he has "some authority under the King." "Which King?" demands Pistol. "Speak, or die." And Falstaff at last learns that Hal, his "tender lambkins," now rules England.

Sir John has visions of grandeur. He orders Bardolph to saddle his horse and excitedly promises Shallow and Pistol high honors. At this climactic moment, Silent, having passed out, is carried to his bed. Then Falstaff, announcing that he is "Fortune's Steward," commands Bardolph to take any available horse, for he, Sir John, "holds all the laws at his commandment." Blessed are his friends, he concludes, but woe to the Lord Chief Justice! Pistol, in his own extravagant style, adds his malediction on England's custodian of law and order as all leave the stage.

CHARACTERS IN SCENE 3

FALSTAFF — Sir John, completely at ease in a situation where he is afforded good food and an abundance of wine. He reaches the highest point in his career when he learns that Hal is King of England.

SHALLOW — Justice-of-the-Peace and squire of Gloucestershire, now flourishing as the expansive, affable host.

SILENT — Kinsman of Shallow and himself a justice-of-the-peace. Thanks to the virtues of wine, he becomes the life of the party.

BARDOLPH — Falstaff's serving man.

THE PAGE — Falstaff's little servant.

DAVY — Shallow's serving man.

PISTOL — One of Falstaff's cronies, here functioning as the messenger in the comic subplot. He is given a fine chance to employ startling expressions culled from the more sensational plays of the era.

PURPOSE OF THE SCENE

1. To bring to a climax the action of the comic subplot.
2. To provide, at the comic level, significant elements of contrast in relation to the main plot, notably the action in the preceding scene.

SUGGESTED QUESTIONS

1. Why is Falstaff so sure that the new King is "sick" for him?
2. What is implied by Falstaff's identification of himself with King Cophetua (line 106)?
3. Is there any special significance in the words of Silent's third ballad (line 77-79)?

ACT V — SCENE 4

SYNOPSIS

Two beadles draw the loudly protesting Hostess Quickly and Doll Tearsheet across the stage, not without difficulty. The Hostess insists that the Second Beadle has dislocated her shoulder and says that she would die to see him hanged. From the words of the First Beadle it is learned that Doll is to receive the punishment of a convicted prostitute — a public whipping. Already established as the mistress of invective, she has a choice collection of scurrilous

52

epithets for him and claims that, as a result of his rough handling, she may lose her unborn child. The Hostess fervently expresses the wish that Sir John Falstaff were present: "He would make this a bloody day to somebody." But she also hopes that Doll does miscarry. The First Beadle scornfully remarks that, if Doll did so, she would have a full dozen cushions. Doll adds more invective and, ordered to move along, she demands to be brought to justice. The Hostess has not remained silent by any means. She deplores the alleged fact that such righteous people should suffer. Her last words inevitably include a malapropism.

CHARACTERS IN SCENE 4

HOSTESS QUICKLY — Owner of the disreputable Boar's-Head Tavern in Eastcheap. Now in dire straits, she continues to mix up words in a comic fashion.

DOLL TEARSHEET — Prostitute at the Boar's-Head, as voluble and scurrilous as ever.

BEADLES — Minor correction officers, responsible to local constables.

CHARACTER MENTIONED BUT NOT PRESENT

SIR JOHN — Falstaff, hero of Mistress Quickly and Doll Tearsheet.

PURPOSE OF THE SCENE

1. To contribute to the resolution of the comic subplot.
2. To show how order is being restored at all levels of society.

SUGGESTED QUESTIONS

1. Why should Hostess Quickly express the wish that Doll Tearsheet miscarry?

2. What does the First Beadle mean when he says to Doll: "If you do, you shall have a dozen cushions again" (lines 16-17)?

3. Why does the First Beadle call Doll a "she knight errant" (line 25)?

ACT V – SCENE 5
SYNOPSIS

Near Westminster Abbey, two grooms strew rushes on the streets, evidence that an important event impends. It is to be the Coronation of Henry V, as one of the grooms states. Falstaff enters with Shallow, Pistol, Bardolph, and the Page. He is all confidence as he assures the gullible Shallow that Henry will be overjoyed to see his old companion. He regrets that he had not had time to use part of the one thousand pounds he had gotten from Shallow: he and members of his group, stained by travel, need new liveries. But, he says, he had ridden hard day and night to prove his affection for the new King. At this point in the action Shallow is the complete yes-man as far as Falstaff is concerned, for he expects at least to be knighted. When Pistol reports that Doll Tearsheet is in prison, the confident Sir John promises to arrange for her prompt release.

Shouts and the sound of trumpets announce the arrival of King Henry V. Prominent among his followers is the Lord Chief Justice. Falstaff and Pistol greet the King effusively. Seeing the knight, Henry instructs the Chief Justice to reprove him. Falstaff, incredulous, again addresses Henry: "My King! My Jove! I speak to thee, my heart!" And then Henry speaks the chilling words: "I know thee not, old man." He lectures his old companion of earlier, carefree days severely, making reference to Falstaff's buffoonery, so indecorous in a white-haired old man; his gluttony; and his neglect of his soul. Warning Sir John not to reply to him "with a fool-born jest," he pronounces sentence, instructing the Lord Chief Justice to see that it is carried out. Falstaff is banished. He is not to come within ten miles of the King on pain of death. But Henry informs Falstaff that he will provide a competence so that the knight will not resort to trickery to raise money. Further, he states, Falstaff will not lack advancement if he truly reforms.

After the King and others leave, Falstaff and Shallow converse. Sir John admits that, so far at least, he has failed to earn the one thousand pounds his friend had given him. But he insists that he will arrange to see the new King privately and that Shallow will be given royal preferment. Shallow, however, is now completely disillusioned. Although Falstaff declares that the King was merely pretending to dismiss his old friend, Shallow remains unconvinced.

As the group are about to leave for dinner, Prince John and the Lord Chief Justice enter, accompanied by officers of the Crown. On the orders of the Chief Justice, Falstaff and his companions are led away to prison. Pistol, in character to the last, revives a Latin tag he had used on an earlier, happier occasion: fortune having deserted him, hope alone remains.

At the end of the scene, Prince John and the Lord Chief Justice hold the stage. Both express their approval of the King's actions. Finally, the audience learns that Henry has called for the assembly of Parliament and, in all probability, will soon lead an invasion of France.

CHARACTERS IN SCENE 5

FALSTAFF—The roistering companion of Henry's madcap days, described by the new King as "The tutor and feeder of my riots." The fat knight at last learns that his wit will not serve him. His basic lack of good judgment and, for that matter, his vanity, are clearly set forth in this scene.

HENRY V—The now completely reformed and dignified ruler of England. Here he is presented as the public justicer passing sentence on a leading representative of disorder in his kingdom. If he appears to some to be unduly cold and severe, it is to be recalled that he does not leave Falstaff destitute, nor does he close the door on the knight's possible restoration.

THE LORD CHIEF JUSTICE—Now one of the strong supports of a King determined to uphold the law, he remains the very symbol of order in the realm.

LANCASTER—Prince John, Duke of Lancaster, brother of Henry V.

SHALLOW—Robert Shallow of Gloucestershire, who has paid a steep price for his trust in Sir John Falstaff and for his own ambition to gain social advancement.

PISTOL—Falstaff's crony and "lieutenant."

CHARACTER NOT PRESENT BUT MENTIONED

DOLL—Doll Tearsheet, the unfortunate prostitute of the Boar's-Head Tavern and one of Falstaff's great admirers.

PURPOSE OF THE SCENE

1. To provide the resolution of the entire action, main plot and sub-plot, in a play the basic theme of which is disorder versus order.
2. To complete the picture of a reformed young Henry,

who now justifies himself by acts, not merely by promises.

3. To prepare the way for *The Life of King Henry the Fifth,* the next English chronicle history written by Shakespeare.

SUGGESTED QUESTIONS

1. Why does Henry V call for the prompt meeting of Parliament?

2. What does the King mean when he says to Falstaff: "...I do despise my dream" (line 55)?

3. What is the implication of the varied terms Falstaff uses successively in his address to the King (44-50)?

SUMMARIES OF LEADING CHARACTERS

HENRY IV—In this play the titular hero, who does not make his appearance until late in the play, although frequent reference is made to him, is much as he was in Act I, Scene 1, of the earlier play. He is a man worn by the cares and troubles of ruling an England torn by civil dissension. He is also a man who is tortured by the knowledge that he himself had been a rebel—that he had deposed Richard II and been responsible for his death. There is abundant evidence that he had been a strong leader, one gifted with the "specialty of rule," to use the sixteen-century term. This is apparent in the counsel he gives to Thomas of Clarence and more particularly to Prince Henry, and in the latter's words to his dying father. If he had aroused the animosities of Northumberland, Scroop, Mowbray and others, he nevertheless had attracted the unwavering loyalty of men like Westmoreland and Warwick. Henry is anything but the cold politician in this play. His concern for the welfare of England is very real and is reflected especially in his worry about the character of his son and heir. He has earned the affection and respect of Henry the younger, as of his three other sons. Nor must one ignore the import of the Lord Chief Justice's words of tribute to the man he long had served. But it is particularly as the grief-stricken father of a son whom he believes to be ungrateful and undisciplined that Henry IV makes his strongest appeal.

PRINCE HENRY—Although Hal appears chiefly in the scenes of the comic subplot, he is never the madcap youth who ignores responsibility. Instead, he is an unusually poised and gifted young man, the breadth of whose character is emphasized again and again. The key to understanding his behavior is, in large part, to be found in the Earl of Warwick's comforting words addressed to the despairing King (IV. iv. 67 ff.). The Prince chose to associate with Falstaff, Poins, and the rest of the riotous crew who made the Boar's-Head their headquarters as a part of his education for kingship. For this is the man who, as Henry V, will move freely among his encamped soldiers in France, conversing easily and understandingly with them. It comes as no surprise to the audience that he should honor the Lord Chief Justice and banish Falstaff. Nor were these actions intended as surprises. Even before Hal made his appearance in this play, the words of the Hostess point to the fact that he would tolerate no disrespect for the King. It will be recalled that he struck Falstaff for making derogatory remarks about Henry IV. In so doing, Hal was acting not only as a dutiful son but as a loyal subject. King Henry IV, convinced that his eldest son's "headstrong riot" will have no curb, acknowledges elements of superiority in Hal's character: the heir-apparent is gracious, sympathetic, charitable. Further evidence of his breadth is his capacity to criticize himself. Just as he is always aware of Falstaff's intentions, so he knows what are the implications of his own actions. Intellectual depth is apparent in his philosophical reflections on what the Crown entails, which are to be taken at their face value. Finally, the all-encompassing virtue of magnanimity in Hal's character is revealed in his solemn promise to his dying father and in his gracious speech to the Lord Chief Justice.

SIR JOHN FALSTAFF—The credits in Falstaff's character are sufficiently impressive, and one can understand why Prince Hal found him so entertaining. His brilliant wit and contagious high spirits make it altogether too easy, perhaps, to ignore the debits. Who is likely to forget such comic descriptions as those of the Gloucester recruits and of Justice Shallow, or such sparkling verbal exercises as his soliloquy on the virtues of wine? He cannot be dismissed as merely a buffoon. For one thing, he has a great fund of knowledge. In his spontaneous discourse he shows close familiarity with the Bible, secular literature, formal logic, music— indeed all the subjects appropriate to a member of the upper classes in Shakespeare's day. It is to be remembered that, as Justice Shallow said, Falstaff had been a page in the household of the first Duke of Norfolk, and that was one of the ways in which the sons of aristocrats were educated. Further, he had attended one of the law schools in London, the pre-requisite for which was university training. And he is *Sir* John Falstaff, a knight of the realm.

Yet Falstaff has chosen to close his eyes on the fact that rank has its obligations. If he indeed possesses much knowledge, he lacks wisdom, basic sound judgment. It has been said that he is a "knave without malice." But malice, or something very close to it, is apparent in his boastful exclamation after learning that Hal is now King of England: "...woe to my Lord Chief Justice!" Contempt for public justice is basic in his character, and it manifests itself not only in his attitude toward the Lord Chief Justice but in his capitalizing on the credulity of such lowly individuals as Mistress Ursula and Hostess Quickly. In the Bible, which Falstaff knew sufficiently well to include many allusions in his discourse, he may have read:

...he who possesses justice lays hold of her and she meets him as an honorable mother. With the bread of life and understanding she feeds him, and gives him the water of wholesome wisdom to drink...

(Ecclus. 15, 1-3)

But Falstaff preferred sack; he cared nothing for the water of wholesome wisdom. Little wonder, then, that he should be completely incredulous when Henry V denounces and banishes him.

Glutton, lecher, parasite, braggart, liar, "great fool," — each of these terms of opporbrium are applicable to Falstaff. However amusing he may be as, for a time, he flourishes as the privileged jester to the Prince, one cannot ignore this fact. It is typical of him that, while officers of the Crown wait for his leadership, he sends Bardolph to fetch Doll Tearsheet to him. For Falstaff, the incomparably amusing Falstaff, is a rebel — a traitor to law and order.

PRINCE JOHN, DUKE OF LANCASTER — The role of this third son of Henry IV is not one which invites the sympathy of modern audiences. But, like the Lord Chief Justice, in a different way, he is presented as the relentless foe of disorder in the kingdom. His determined attitude toward the northern insurgents and his sound estimate of Falstaff's behavior mark him as one devoted to public duty. He is not depicted as a warm, human person like his gifted elder brother, Prince Hal. But he must be recognized as a pillar of law and order. In this respect he fulfils his function in the play.

THE EARL OF WESTMORELAND — He is one of the characters who, in his capacity as Prince John's emissary to the rebels, functions as the voice of political orthodoxy in this play: no subject, however exalted, has the right to "lift an angry arm" against God's representative on earth, the King. Unflinchingly he carries out the order of his superior; it is he who places the rebels under arrest for treason at the end of the parley at Gaultree Forest in Yorkshire.

MOWBRAY — The second Duke of Norfolk is an astute and courageous warrior who had proved his worth. From one point of view his action contrasts with that of the pusillanimous Earl of Northumberland, who fears to commit himself in the struggle against

Henry IV. From another point of view, he provides a contrast to the unrealistic Lord Hastings and even the Archbishop of York, who in his optimism, rejects Mowbray's sound counsel.

THE EARL OF NORTHUMBERLAND — The elder Henry Percy is depicted as one who is at first determined to avenge himself upon Henry IV after the defeat at Shrewsbury and the death of his son. But he emerges as one who is concerned primarily about his own safety and welfare. His action of abandoning the Yorkshire rebels is consistent with his convenient absenting himself from the conflict at Shrewsbury, as dramatized in *Henry IV, Part I*.

THE ARCHBISHOP OF YORK — Richard Scroop is a man who owed his advancement to high ecclesiastical office to Richard II and who never forgets that Henry IV was the one who ordered the execution of his brother. He is the determined leader of the active rebel force in the north parts. But it is not merely personal grievances that motivate his bold challenge of the Crown. His consideration and acceptance of the terms offered by Prince John indicate that basically he is a man of good will, anxious to bring a just settlement to issues which have led him to rebel against the King.

LORD CHIEF JUSTICE OF THE KING'S BENCH — He is not without mellow good humor, as is evident in his first exchange with Falstaff in this play. Indeed, some commentators go so far as to say that he really enjoys plump Jack as much as anyone else. Yet basically he is the noble, serious pillar of the law, properly devoted to the execution of justice. That he had not hesitated to punish Prince Hal is sufficient proof of his moral courage. It will be noted that the newly crowned Henry V repeats the essential charges against Falstaff that the Lord Chief Justice had made earlier in the play. His courage is no less apparent in his apologia, spoken in the belief that the new King was about to excoriate him and remove him from office. Of all the characters in the play he is the one eminently fitted to be the "father" of King Henry V's youth.

WARWICK — Richard de Beauchamp, Earl of Warwick, remains almost constantly at the side of Henry IV, serving as the trusted and capable counsellor and attendant. In this play he is remembered especially for his insight into the character of Prince Hal when he seeks to reassure the troubled King. Yet late in the play he joins those who fear that Hal will not follow the wise path of his father.

LORD HASTINGS — One of the representatives of the northern aristocrats who actively opposed the rule of Henry IV, he proves to be a bad counsellor to the Archbishop of York, for he is over-confident and easily deceived by the royalist leaders. He thus provides an interesting contrast to the sagacious Mowbray.

BARDOLPH — Falstaff's serving man proves his worth to his master in numerous ways. Under instructions, he attempts to underwrite the knight's credit with tradesman; he is ready to draw his sword when Fang, the sheriff's officer, declares Falstaff to be under arrest; and he expertly carries out the business of accepting bribes from the Gloucestershire recruits. But his greatest contribution is his physical appearance. His flaming nose continues to inspire witty comment as it did in *Henry IV, Part I*.

PISTOL — A "humours" character, that is, one who has a special idiosyncrasy which makes him ridiculous, he serves as emissary to Falstaff, who ironically addresses him as "Captain Pistol." Perhaps some find his ranting rather monotonous, but there is sufficient evidence that Elizabethans were vastly amused by this broad satire on the verbal excesses in popular tragedies and melodramas. He reappears in *Henry V*. Doll Tearsheet, whose favors he had enjoyed, has the best epithets for him: he is "a swaggering rascal," a "fustian rascal," a "bottle-ale rascal." And, of course, he is a coward.

POINS — One of the regulars at the Boar's-Head Tavern, with whom Prince Hal chooses to associate for a time, he functions in this play much as he did in *Henry IV, Part I*. It is he who devises the plot to entrap Sir John Falstaff, who is jealous because the Prince shows Poins some favor. Poins is sufficiently skilful in witty conversation, but it is primarily his ingenuity in devising practical jokes that has attracted the Prince.

SHALLOW — Master Robert Shallow, Esquire, the Gloustershire justice-of-the-peace, is essentially a caricature — and a good one. He does share two things with Falstaff. He had been a student at one of the London law schools; and he is ambitious to capitalize upon his friendship. But there identity with Sir John ends. He indeed is a shallow man. One does not laugh with him, as one often does with Falstaff, but at him. The poverty of his mind is revealed time and again. For example, it is he who boasts of wild escapades in his youthful days, who is impelled to explain Falstaff's joke on Ralph Mouldy's name, and who pontificates when Pistol arrives with important news for Sir John. His vanity is no less apparent, again with reference to his alleged youthful wildness and in his reminding all present that he has some authority from the King. His garrulity, his uncertain memory of times past, and his tendency to introduce irrelevancies contribute notably to the comedy in this play. In his person Shakespeare also satirizes the country justice who makes the most of his local authority and is easily influenced by any close associate to modify legal decisions.

SILENT — Kinsman of the wispy Shallow, the bare-bones

Silent, himself a justice-of-the peace, provides an amusing contrast to the loquacious squire. At first he contributes nothing but unspoken admiration of Shallow. But later the wine extolled by Falstaff works its wonders, and Silent distinguishes himself as the singer of popular ballads and the frank commentator on Sir John himself.

MISTRESS QUICKLY—Hostess of the Boar's-Head Tavern and, according to Falstaff, a widow, she is among those victimized by Sir John. She endears herself to the audience chiefly because of her genius for misusing big words of which she is so fond. Despite the fact that the audience first meets her in this play in the act of demanding the arrest of Falstaff, the latter remains her hero. And her affection for him actually points to the fact that she also embraces disorder. Among other things, she is a procuress, and her protestations of respectability are rather pathetic. It is from this point of view that one should interpret the action in her last scene, wherein she is dragged off to prison.

DOLL TEARSHEET—Falstaff's Helen of Troy, as Pistol calls her, is another representative of unlicensed behavior. Prince Hal and Poins describe her accurately enough at the end of Act II, Scene 3. Indeed she "should be some road," one "as common as the way between St. Albans and London." If she reserves a special place in her affections for Falstaff, her favors remain for hire even to the likes of Pistol. She is generally depicted as a harridan addicted to shrill vocal outbursts.

GENERAL NOTES

DURATION OF THE ACTION

Shakespeare, the poet-dramatist, telescopes the events of history in this play as in the other chronicle-histories. If he did not do so he would not have achieved drama. Henry IV endured troubles with the Welsh and with France, which are referred to but not dramatized in this play, and with the Lollards (native religious protestants), and with Scotland. But he confines his attention for dramatic purposes to the northern insurgents. The following brief summary of the actual time schedule of historical events may give a good insight into the dramatist's method of adapting historical material to his purpose.

Rumors and authentic reports of what happened at Shrewsbury belong to the year 1403. Two years later the rebellion led by the Archbishop of York occurred. It was not until 1409 that, as recorded by Holinshed, Owen Glendower, leader of the belligerent Welsh, died. The meeting at Gaultree Forest in Yorkshire, followed by the arrest of the rebel leaders, took place in 1405. Three years later the Earl of Northumberland and Lord Bardolph were defeated by the royalists and sent to their deaths. King Henry IV fell ill in 1412 and survived until 1413. Shakespeare, obviously, compresses the events of years into a few weeks and days for "the two hours traffic" of his stage.

MEDIUM: VERSE AND PROSE

Shakespeare employs verse almost entirely in the serious parts of the play, and prose almost entirely elsewhere. Out of a total of 3446 lines, 1860 are in prose. This is a clear indication that, in contrast to *Henry IV, Part I,* the comic scenes are dominant, at least in playing time, in the later play which concerns us.

Blank verse, that is, unrhymed iambic pentameter, belongs especially to the main plot wherein the very fate of the realm is the issue. Such verse is necessarily formal, an idealization of ordinary discourse. One way in which the poet emphasizes the high rank of a given speaker and the seriousness of the immediate action is to employ this medium. Often it is highly rhetorical, as when the Earl of Northumberland gives way to grief and rage in Act I, Scene i. To apply the standrads of realistic and naturalistic discourse to such lines is to miss the point entirely. So elsewhere in the plot. Such formalization and idealizing are especially apparent in such speeches as those by Westmoreland and Prince John when they address the rebel leaders. Nor would it do to reject blank verse in the scenes in which Henry IV appears. But if such verse is often highly rhetorical, Shakespeare avoids the excesses which, indeed, he satirized, in the bombastic outbursts of Pistol. Moreover, at this advanced state in his creative life, he used blank verse with increasing freedom so as to provide a more natural tone to speeches. One way of doing this is to write lines which admit no pause at the end of the line. And this run-on effect is made possible especially by the use of terminal words which are not accented on the last syllable. Compare the following lines (IV. iv. 3-6):

We will our youth lead on to higher fields
And draw no swords but what are sanctified.

So far the pause is at the end of each line, and the last word is accented on the final syllable.

Our Navy is addressed, our powers collected,
Our substitutes in absence well invested...

In these lines, which immediately follow the first two, the final syllables are unaccented so that, despite the punctuation, the sense runs on from the first to the second line naturally, as in ordinary discourse.

A second way of avoiding excessive formality recommended itself to Shakespeare. Frequently a speech ends short of a complete line of verse, and the opening words of the next speaker complete the line. Consider the lines at the very beginning of the play:

> *L. Bar.* Who keeps the gate here, ho?
> Where is the Earl?
>   *Por.* What shall I say you are?
>   *L. Bar.*   Tell thou the Earl
> That the Lord Bardolph doth attend him here.

Rhymed iambic pentameter couplets are used eighty-four times in the play. They occur at the end of many speeches, as when Prince Henry refers to the crown in reply to his father (IV. v. 221-225):

> My gracious liege,
> You won it, wore it, kept it, gave it me.
> Then plain and right must my possession be,
> Which I with more than with a common pain
> 'Gainst all the world will rightfully maintain.

Typically, rhyming couplets are used at the end of the last speech in scenes of the main plot. Thus at the end of Act I, Scene I, Northumberland says:

> Get posts and letters, and make friends with speed.
> Never so few, and never yet more need.

The couplets provide special emphasis, a particular kind of climax; often they are epigrammatic.

By the time he came to write the *Henry IV* plays, Shakespeare habitually used prose for comic scenes. Falstaff, appropriately, is a speaker of prose. And when it is the comic element which is to the fore, Prince Hal and all others speak in prose. Since Falstaff is hardly the conquering hero, it would not do to have him use blank verse as the chief medium even in Act IV, Scene 3, wherein Sir John "captures" Colevile of the Dale; and addressing the knight, Prince John also speaks in prose. But, it will be noted, when the Prince turns to the Earl of Westmoreland, he shifts to blank verse. So elsewhere in the play, whenever serious matters relating to the main action are introduced. At the end of the comic tavern scene, Act II, Scene 2, Peto enters with important news for Prince Hal and Falstaff. He speaks lines of blank verse, as does Prince Hal in reply.

One should recognize that there is a wide range in the kinds of prose used in this play. Falstaff can be as colloquial as anyone. "Whose mare's dead?" he asks when he makes his first appearance in Act II, Scene 1. And he can more than hold his own with Prince Hal in sparkling prose that has the very rhythm and sophistication of upper class discourse. The fact that he often calls a spade a spade should not blind one to this fact. Take the following dialogue, for example (II. iv. 352 ff.):

Prince. See now whether pure fear and entire cowardice doth not make thee wrong this virtuous gentlewoman to close with us. Is she of the wicked? Is thine hostess here of the wicked? Or is thy boy of the wicked? Or honest Bardolph, whose zeal burns in his nose, of the wicked?

Poins. Answer, thou dead elm, answer.

Fal. The Fiend hath pricked down Bardolph irrecover- able, and his face is Lucifer's privy kitchen, where he doth nothing but roast maltworms. For the boy, there is a good angel about him, but the Devil outbids him too.

The ranting of Pistol, the billingsgate of Doll Tearsheet, and the simple, realistic talk of Shallow and Silence further illustrate the wide range in the prose style. So great is Shakespeare's reputation as premier poet that perhaps not enough credit is given to him as a writer of superior prose at all levels.

SIXTEENTH-CENTURY
POLITICAL THEORY

Since *Henry IV, Parts I and II,* are political plays, it is neces- sary to understand the political doctrine behind them if one is to do justice to Shakespeare's intentions. Elizabeth I, the fifth Tudor to rule England, had come to a throne which was in many ways insecure because of rival claims. Henry VIII, her father, had found it especially necessary to inculcate the doctrine of absolute obed- ience to the Crown after the break with Rome in 1536. During his reign he had experienced the Pilgrimage of Grace, a rebellion in northern England; and later the Exeter Conspiracy, an alleged attempt to depose Henry VIII and to place a Yorkist on the throne of England. After Henry VIII's death, England endured the Western Rebellion of 1549. And during Elizabeth's reign there occurred the Rebellion of 1569, as well as plots against the Queen's life, notably the Babington Plot, which led to the trial, conviction, and execution of Mary, Queen of Scots. Throughout the century and beyond,

England had reason to fear an invasion and the rising of native Catholics: the danger was by no means restricted to the year 1588, when Philip II of Spain sent his Armada to subdue England. In view of such challenges to Tudor supremacy, there was a need of a political philosophy which would prevent challenges to royal authority and devastating civil war. The basic arguments were developed during the reign of Henry VIII and augmented as new crises arose during the reigns of Edward VI and Elizabeth I. It found expression in officially approved pamphlet and tract, and in belletristic literature, notably drama and non-dramatic poetry. Especially it was emphasized in official sermons, the first group of which was introduced in the year 1549. These included strongly worded instruction on the subject of obedience. They were augmented in 1570, following the Rebellion of 1569 and the papal decree of excommunication of Queen Elizabeth I. Every Englishman was required to hear the sermons on obedience three times during the year. The gist of the doctrine was this: the ruler was God's lieutenant on earth; no subject, however exalted, had the right actively to oppose him. To do so was a sin against religion, punishable by suffering here and now and by eternal damnation after death. Even if the ruler is a tyrant, the subject had no right to oppose him, for the head of the state was the anointed representative of God on earth. In support of this doctrine, appeals were made primarily to Biblical authority. Texts such as Romans xiii and Proverbs viii, as well as ones in the Gospel according to St. Matthew, were cited repeatedly. John of Gaunt, Duke of Lancaster, summed up the doctrine concisely in his response to his sister-in-law, the Duchess of Gloucester, who reminded him that the reigning King, Richard II, had been responsible for the death of her husband and Gaunt's brother:

> God's is the quarrel, for God's substitute,
> His deputy anointed in His sight,
> Hath caused his death. The which if wrongfully,
> Let Heaven revenge, for I may never lift
> An angry arm against his minister.
> *(Richard II,* Act II, Scene 2, lines 37-41)

That Henry IV should so suffer is to be explained by the fact that he, son of John of Gaunt, did "lift an angry arm against [God's] minister." He endures rebellion; he sees the apparent waywardness of Prince Hal as part of his punishment; he does not live to lead a new crusade against the foes of Christianity and thus do penance for his grievous sins. But, according to sixteenth-century Tudor political theory, he wore the crown on God's sufferance, no one had the right to oppose him. All this should make understandable the words of indictment spoken first by the Earl of Westmoreland and later by Prince John to a high church dignitary who had turned rebel, the Archbishop of York. It should illuminate further the apparently despicable behavior of Prince John, who, after tricking the rebel leaders, sends each to death—even the admirable Sir John Colevile of the Dale. In Prince John's words, "God, and not we, hath safely fought today."

QUESTIONS AND ANSWERS

1. QUESTION: How would you describe the character of Henry V as he appears in Act V?

ANSWER: He is now the ideal ruler. In Scene 5 he assures his brothers that he will surround himself with wise counsellors and that his reign will be second to none in its reputation for justice and wisdom. It is his reconciliation with the Lord Chief Justice of the King's Bench, a man with whom he had had difficulties earlier, which is the dramatic representation of his avowed intentions. In his rejection of Falstaff, we have complete evidence that he will indeed govern in accordance with the principles of law and order.

2. QUESTION: What evidence do we have of Shallow's ambitions to become at least a knight of the realm?

ANSWER: He is first presented as the local big-wig, now in his dotage, who boasts of his youthful exploits and who is something of a name-dropper. He speaks of his comradeship with Sir John Falstaff, who was once a page in the household of the eminent first Duke of Norfolk. On Falstaff's testimony we know that he speaks glibly of John of Gaunt, son of Edward III and father of Henry IV. He is indeed the affable host, but he obviously has an axe to grind. The dead give-away is the snatch of song sung by Silent (V. iii. 77-79):

Do me right,
And dub me knight.
Samingo.

And it is Shallow himself who assures Silent that it is well to have a friend who is influential at Court, and he is at pains to make it clear that he is "under the King, in some authority."

3. QUESTION: What is Falstaff's defense of himself and of his way of life?

ANSWER: At least an entire chapter could be written on this subject, but in brief the following are essential points. First, he correctly states that he is "not only witty in [himself] but the cause of wit in other men." To the Lord Chief Justice he insists that he is indeed old, but only in wisdom and judgment, the fruits of long experience. As the intimate of the heir-apparent, he knows how to amuse the Prince. Reflecting on how he will gull Justice Shallow and how he will use this experience to regale the Prince and thus maintain his status as privileged jester, Falstaff reflects that "a lie with a slight oath and a jest with a sad brow will do with a fellow that never had an ache in his shoulders"—that is, a young man unafflicted with rheumatism.

4. QUESTION: What are the functions of the soliloquies in this play and who speaks them?

ANSWER: The soliloquy is one of the long-lived conventions of drama which Shakespeare found particularly useful. The term itself comes from the Latin word *solus,* meaning "alone." A character in a play may occupy the stage alone and speak his thoughts for the benefit of the audience. Thus the audience may be given a penetrating insight into the character of the speaker or may learn the motives for an action. Again it may provide a commentary on the character of others in the play or give details relating to antecedent action.

Both Falstaff and Prince Hal deliver soliloquies. Sir John's first one appears at the end of Act I, Scene 1, and is just six lines long. But from it we get a good insight into his character: he is a man who is confident that his wit will make it possible for him to capitalize even on afflictions. Elsewhere (III.ii.323 ff. and V.ii. 69-95), his prose soliloquies tell us a great deal about Shallow and just as much about himself. His greatest and longest soliloquy occurs near the end of Act IV, Scene 3 (lines 92-135). This is his rilliant discourse on the virtues of wine, in which Falstaff contributes much to the understanding of Prince Hal and Prince John.

Prince Hal's memorable soliloquy occurs in Act IV, Scene 5, as he contemplates the crown resting on a pillow near his sleeping father. From his words we understand his true motive for removing the crown and placing it on his head and an insight into the serious side of the Prince's character. Further, we are made increasingly aware of the great responsibilities which he must face when he becomes King of England.

5. QUESTION: What does Prince Hal mean when he says to Poins: "Let the end try the man" (II. ii. 50)?

ANSWER: A man must be judged by the final outcome of his actions. In this line Shakespeare gives the audience a clear indication of the Prince's intentions. It is one of the passages which look forward to the rejection of Falstaff.

6. QUESTION: What is the purpose of the epilogue to the play?

ANSWER: Traditionally, an epilogue is the last division of a formal speech. In plays it is usually added as the plea of an actor for sympathetic treatment by the audience. Shakespeare used seven epilogues; but the one in *Henry IV, Part II,* is unique because it contains an apology. From the lines spoken by the Dancer, it is apparent that an unidentified play had given offense by introducing the name of Sir John Oldcastle, an actual historical personage whose descendants survived. This was Falstaff's earlier name, and it survives, in a sense, when Prince Hal addresses Sir John as "my old lad of the castle" *(Henry IV, Part I,* Act I, Scene 2, lines 47-48). Of interest also is the fact that, according to the Epilogue, Shakespeare originally planned to find a place for Falstaff in his next chronicle history play, *Henry V.* When he came to write that play, however, he did no more than to report Falstaff's death.

7. QUESTION: What reason had Henry IV to be now confident, now disconsolate as regards his successor?

ANSWER: He takes comfort in the knowledge that his son will inherit the crown from the father. He is convinced that those who personally opposed him, knowing that Richard II had willed the throne to Edmund Mortimer, will not oppose a king who was not guilty of usurpation. But in view of Prince Hal's lapses in conduct after the Battle of Shrewsbury and his return from Wales, he feels that his son will make mistakes as fatal as those which cost Richard II life and crown.

8. QUESTION: What is the meaning of the following lines of advice spoken by King Henry IV to Thomas of   Clarence (IV.iv.41-48):

> Learn this, Thomas,
> And thou shalt prove a shelter to thy friends,
> A hoop of gold to bind thy brothers in,
> That the united vessel of their blood,
> Mingled with venom of suggestion—
> As, perforce, the age will pour it in—
> Shall never leak, though it do work as strong
> As aconitum or rash gunpowder.

ANSWER: The King has urged Thomas of Clarence to study the complex character of the heir-apparent, who particularly favors him. The image in this passage is that of a cask. Thomas' other brothers are the staves and Thomas himself is the hoop which holds them together. The "venom of suggestion" is the malicious accusations and slanders of the envious. Such "venom" will test the strength of the cask, which should be able to withstand weather, poison, or discharge from weapons.

9. QUESTION: Compare the characters of the Earl of Northumberland and the Archbishop of York.

ANSWER: The Earl breaks forth in stormy passion when he learns of the defeat and his son's death at Shrewsbury, and it would seem that nothing will stop him from seeking revenge at once. Actually, however, he is a man who talks bravely enough on occasion but fails miserably when put to the test. Shakespeare followed Holinshed in suggesting that the Earl remained "crafty sick" at Warkworth Castle rather than joining his son and his brother at Shrewsbury. Although he had given his solemn pledge to lead forces in support of those raised by the Archbishop of York, he is easily persuaded to fly to Scotland and to remain there until he learned how the Yorkist rebels fared. The inescapable conclusion is that the Earl of Northumberland depends upon outward show and lacks basic integrity.

In contrast, the Archbishop of York, however mistaken he may be in his efforts and wrong in his judgment as regards Prince John's intentions, is a courageous and honest man. It is true that he had a personal grievance against King Henry IV, who had been responsible for the execution of his brother. But as Shakespeare depicts him, the Archbishop's reasons for leading an armed revolt transcend personal issues. This is evident in the fact that he had prepared articles of grievances and endeavored to get redress prior to the rising, and that he readily accepted the terms offered by Prince John. There is no indication that lack of confidence in the strength and ability of the rebel force led him to capitulate. He received the news of Northumberland's flight without thought of retreat. Finally, he had won and held the loyalty of such men as Mowbray, Lord Hastings, and Sir John Colevile of the Dale.

10. QUESTION: What is the meaning of Shallow's reference to himself as once having been "Sir Dagonet in Arthur's show"?

ANSWER: Arthur's show was an archery exhibition put on by a group of men who assumed the names of King Arthur's knights. Since Sir Dagonet was the court fool in the Arthurian stories, it is only fitting that Shallow should have had that name.

NOTES

NOTES

NOTES

NOTES